Advance Praise for *Why Software Sucks . . .*

"I've just finished reading the best computer book [*Why Software Sucks*] since I last re-read one of mine and I wanted to pass along the good word. . . . Put this one on your must-have list if you have software, love software, hate programmers, or even ARE a programmer, because Mr. Platt (who teaches programming) has set out to puncture the bloated egos of all those who think that just because they can write a program, they can make it easy to use. . . . This book is funny, but it is also an important wake-up call for software companies that want to reduce the size of their customer support bills. If you were ever stuck for an answer to the question, 'Why do good programmers make such awful software?' this book holds the answer."

— *John McCormick, Locksmith columnist, TechRepublic.com*

"I must say first, I don't get many computing manuscripts that make me laugh out loud. Between the laughs, Dave Platt delivers some very interesting insight and perspective, all in a lucid and engaging style. I don't get much of that either!"

— *Henry Leitner, assistant dean for information technology and senior lecturer on computer science, Harvard University*

"A riotous book for all of us downtrodden computer users, written in language that we understand."

— *Stacy Baratelli, author's barber*

"David's unique take on the problems that bedevil software creation made me think about the process in new ways. If you care about the quality of the software you create or use, read this book."

— *Dave Chappell, principal, Chappell & Associates*

"I began to read it in my office but stopped before I reached the bottom of the first page. I couldn't keep a grin off my face! I'll enjoy it after I go back home and find a safe place to read."

— *Tsukasa Makino, IT manager*

"David explains, in terms that my mother-in-law can understand, why the software we use today can be so frustrating, even dangerous at times, and gives us some real ideas on what we can do about it."

— *Jim Brosseau, Clarrus Consulting Group, Inc.*

Why
Software
SUCKS...

and what you
can do
about it

Why Software SUCKS...

and what you can do about it

DAVID S. PLATT

✦✦ Addison-Wesley

Upper Saddle River, NJ • Boston • Indianapolis • San Francisco
New York • Toronto • Montreal • London • Munich • Paris • Madrid
Capetown • Sydney • Tokyo • Singapore • Mexico City

The publisher offers excellent discounts on this book when ordered in quantity for bulk purchases or special sales, which may include electronic versions and/or custom covers and content particular to your business, training goals, marketing focus, and branding interests. For more information, please contact:

    U.S. Corporate and Government Sales
    (800) 382-3419
    corpsales@pearsontechgroup.com

For sales outside the United States please contact:

    International Sales
    international@pearsoned.com

Visit us on the Web: www.awprofessional.com

Library of Congress Cataloging-in-Publication Data

Platt, David S.
  Why software sucks...and what you can do about it / David S. Platt.
    p. cm.
  ISBN 0-321-46675-6 (pbk. : alk. paper) 1. Computer
software—Development. I. Title.
  QA76.76.D47.P52 2006
  005.3—dc22

                                 2006022500

ISBN 0-321-46675-6

Text printed in the United States on recycled paper at RR Donnelley in Crawfordsville, Indiana.

First printing, September 2006

To my daughters, Lucy Katrina Platt and Annabelle Rose Platt

CONTENTS

• • •

Acknowledgments   xiii

INTRODUCTION   1

1. WHO'RE YOU CALLING A DUMMY?   9

Where We Came From   10

Why It Still Sucks Today   11

Control versus Ease of Use   13

I Don't Care How Your Program Works   15

A Bad Feature and a Good One   19

Stopping the Proceedings with Idiocy   23

Testing on Live Animals   26

Where We Are and What You Can Do   28

2. TANGLED IN THE WEB   31

Where We Came From   32

How It Works   34

Why It Still Sucks Today   37

Client-Centered Design versus Server-Centered Design   40

Where's My Eye Opener?   46

It's Obvious—Not!   52
Splash, Flash, and Animation   56
Testing on Live Animals   59
What You Can Do about It   61

3. KEEP ME SAFE   65
The Way It Was   66
Why It Sucks Today   67
What Programmers Need to Know, but Don't   71
A Human Operation   77
Budgeting for Hassles   80
Users Are Lazy   83
Social Engineering   87
Last Word on Security   92
What You Can Do   93

4. WHO THE HECK ARE YOU?   97
Where We Came From   97
Why It Still Sucks Today   98
Incompatible Requirements   99
OK, So Now What?   106

5. WHO'RE YOU LOOKING AT?   119
Yes, They Know You   119
Why It Sucks More Than Ever Today   122
Users Don't Know Where the Risks Are   125
What They Know First   127
Milk You with Cookies?   129
Privacy Policy Nonsense   138
Covering Your Tracks   140
The Google Conundrum   141
Solution   145

6. TEN THOUSAND GEEKS, CRAZED ON JOLT COLA   149
See Them in Their Native Habitat   149
All These Geeks   150

Who Speaks, and When, and about What 153
Selling It 158
The Next Generation of Geeks — Passing It On 161

7. WHO ARE THESE CRAZY BASTARDS ANYWAY? 169
Homo Logicus 170
Testosterone Poisoning 171
Control and Contentment 173
Making Models 175
Geeks and Jocks 177
Jargon 179
Brains and Constraints 181
Seven Habits of Geeks 183

8. MICROSOFT: CAN'T LIVE WITH 'EM AND CAN'T LIVE WITHOUT 'EM 189
They Run the World 189
Me and Them 190
Where We Came From 193
Why It Sucks Today 195
Damned if You Do, Damned if You Don't 199
We Love to Hate Them 203
Plus ça Change 207
Growing-Up Pains 211
What You Can Do about It 214
The Last Word 220

9. DOING SOMETHING ABOUT IT 223
1. Buy 224
2. Tell 229
3. Ridicule 232
4. Trust 233
5. Organize 237

EPILOGUE 241

ABOUT THE AUTHOR 243

ACKNOWLEDGMENTS

Any book is the product of a team effort. In this one, I've had an outstanding supporting cast. Everyone at Addison-Wesley understood and got behind the concept of a book for the users of computers, not the programmers that they usually deal with. Instead of, "That's not what we do here," they stepped up and said, "Hey, cool, look what we get a chance to do."

First, thanks have to go to my editor, Peter Gordon, who on the initial reading, replied that "I don't get many computing manuscripts that make me laugh out loud." Thanks also to other Addison-Wesley team members, including Curt Johnson, Kim Boedigheimer, Julie Nahil, Audrey Doyle, Anna Popick, and Eric Garulay. And I'll thank my friend and fellow author, David Chappell, for referring me to Addison-Wesley in the first place. I'd also like to thank my agent, Alex Glass of Trident Media Group, and author Catherine Coulter, who referred me to him.

I got the inspiration for this book from reading *Complications: a Surgeon's Notes on an Imperfect Science*, by Atul Gawande, which is a surgeon's inside view of his own profession. I thought to myself, "Hey, I can write this same sort of book about my own profession, software development. And mine'll be funnier." His chapter "9000 Surgeons," about surgeons' behavior at their annual conference, directly led to my chapter "Ten Thousand Geeks, Crazed on Jolt Cola."

xiv · · · WHY SOFTWARE SUCKS

I need to thank all of my friends, coworkers, clients, and students—all the people who read early drafts and gave me good feedback. I learn so much from working with you. And to all the developers who write good software, so I have something to point at and say, "Here, this good thing, that's what we're capable of." And to all the developers of sucky software as well, without whom I'd have nothing to ridicule, and this book wouldn't be nearly as interesting.

Finally, I'd like to thank my family: my wife, Linda; daughters, Annabelle Rose and Lucy Katrina; and cats, Simba, Marley, and Sally.

Why Software SUCKS...

and what you
can do
about it

INTRODUCTION

Today's software sucks. There's no other good way to say it. It's unsafe, allowing criminal programs to creep through the Internet wires into our very bedrooms. It's unreliable, crashing when we need it most, wiping out hours or days of work with no way to get it back. And it's hard to use, requiring large amounts of head banging to figure out the simplest operations.

This isn't news to you, is it? You're not dumb, contrary to what that yellow-and-black book series would have you believe. Today's software really does suck, as you've always thought. That's why you laughed when you read the title of this book. And it wasn't a voluntary laugh, either, was it? You didn't read the title and think to yourself, "Hey, that's kinda funny, I think I'll laugh." No. The title touched a nerve, like a smell knifing through your cerebral cortex to your reptilian midbrain, and you burst out with an involuntary, explosive laugh. When you started thinking again, you probably thought something like, "Hey, cool! Here's a guy (an articulate, credentialed, handsome, and modest one, too, by the look of things) telling it like it is, saying in print what I've always thought. About time, too." Indeed it is. This book explains in nontechnical, jargon-free language exactly how this situation came about, and what you can do to change it. "Damn right I'll buy it! And copies for my friends, too." Excellent idea. Told you that you weren't a dummy, didn't I?

Fifteen years ago—even ten—ordinary people didn't use software in their daily lives. My parents did not send e-mail birthday cards to their granddaughters, or expect me to send them digital photos that way. They balanced their checking accounts on a paper register and maintained their schedules by writing in ink on paper calendars with pretty pictures. The few people who did regularly use software usually had to as part of their jobs—for example, travel agents using airline reservation systems to issue tickets. These people used small, custom-tailored applications that required expensive, proprietary hardware and extensive training and ongoing support and that weren't useful for any other purpose. The World Wide Web was this geeky thing for wooly haired academics. Most people didn't even know it existed, let alone that you could steal music or download dirty pictures from it.

That's changed completely, almost overnight in societal terms, and seemingly without our noticing it. My parents now use a financial software package to manage their checking accounts, which pays bills electronically so that they don't run out of stamps, and automatically shows electronic deposits and cleared checks as they arrive at the bank. Not only do they want granddaughter photos by e-mail, but they're also asking for live streaming video. With unlimited high-speed access available to home users for about $40 per month, the Web has accomplished what proponents of nuclear power predicted and never managed to do, which is become too cheap to meter. It's now so ubiquitous that the state of Pennsylvania has removed its motto, "The Keystone State," from its automobile license plates and replaced it with the state Web address, www.state.pa.us (see Figure 1). Florida has done Pennsylvania one better, keeping its slogan but replacing the state name with the Web address MyFlorida.com (see Figure 2). And the travel agent's profession has been largely wiped out by ordinary people having cheap, easy access to information that once required very expensive and complicated setups.

We live our lives today in a sea of software, but most users have no idea how software comes into being or why it works the way it

FIGURE 1 Pennsylvania state license plate showing Web address rather than state motto

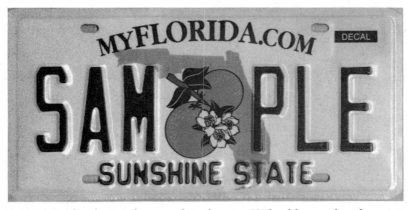

FIGURE 2 Florida state license plate showing Web address rather than state name

does. We only know that we don't like it very much. Everyone has a software horror story or five, just as we have airline horror stories about flights delayed for hours on the runway and luggage mis-routed to Timbuktu. You worked all day with your program, didn't realize you had to explicitly save your document, then that damn program crashed and you lost it all. And the random pattern of bits on your screen looked exactly like it was flipping you the bird as it went down. From *TIME* magazine's 1982 pick as "Man of the Year" the personal computer's reputation has gone downhill. The cartoon "Devolution" expresses most users' feelings very well (see Figure 3).

Software doesn't have to suck, and it shouldn't, but it does. One reason is that the programmers and architects and managers who develop it don't understand their customers anywhere near as well as they should, as well as designers in other industries have been forced to. Their products suck not because developers don't know how to do this or that particular thing, but because they don't know which things to do. They're disconnected from their customers (some would call them victims)—the ones who pay their salaries—and they usually don't realize it. They often solve the wrong problem, adding features that no one cares about except themselves, harming all users in the process. If they understood who their users are, they'd make different, better choices.

For example, Microsoft Office applications such as Word and Excel allow a user to drag the main menu (the one with File, Edit, and Help on it) from its usual location at the top of the window to any other edge of the screen, or even floating free over a document (see Figure 4). I've never met or even heard of anybody, and I mean not one single person, who has ever used this feature, not even my contacts on the Office team. So why does it hurt the program to have it? For many reasons. I occasionally reach my mouse up to

Something, somewhere went terribly wrong

FIGURE 3 Users have changed their minds, now, haven't they?

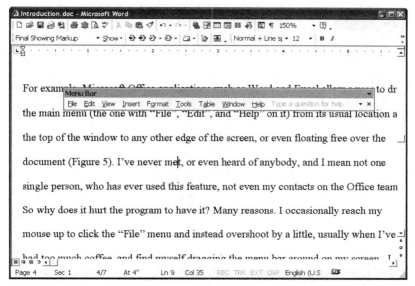

FIGURE 4 Microsoft Word main menu floating free over a document. You can do it, but why would anyone want to?

click the File menu and instead overshoot by a little, usually when I've had too much coffee, and find myself dragging the menu bar around on my screen. I have to stop what I'm doing, drag the bar back where it belongs, dock it in the place where it belongs, above the toolbar; then spend half a minute cursing the ancestry of the morons who wrote this dumb, so-called feature. This might not sound like much, but 30 seconds twice a day, times a billion users, add up to wasting roughly 27 human life spans every single day.[1] I, and the vast majority of users, would be more productive if this feature was completely removed from the program so that we wouldn't waste our time and break our concentration by having to deal with this nonsense. In addition, the extra programming instructions (called "code" by programmers) needed to provide this feature increase the possibility of crashing errors and security vulnerabilities, in the same way as more moving parts on any mechanical

---

1. A billion minutes is 694,444 days, 1,901 years, or just over 27 spans of 70 years.

FIGURE 5 The late, unlamented Clippy

device render it less reliable. The world would be a better place if Microsoft had taken the money it spent on designing, writing, testing, debugging, documenting, and supporting this foolishness and burned it, or better yet, given it to me. Worst of all, these antiproductive doodads consume development resources that could have and should have been spent on items that most users actually do care about, such as falling over dead less often and not losing work when that happens. The ultimate example of resources wasted on counterproductive features is Clippy (see Figure 5), the talking, dancing, irritating paper clip in Microsoft Office (added in 1997, deactivated by popular demand in 2002).[2]

Not only does software suck today, but it will continue to do so until we demand that it stop. Our cars improved in terms of safety (air bags and antilock brakes), reliability (better engineering leading to fewer failures), and usability (CD players and cup holders) only when customers started demanding them, buying cars that had them and passing over those that didn't. My mother always told me not to complain about something unless I had a better idea. I do have many better ideas, and I give them to you as I point out the foolishness of some current software design decisions. While this isn't primarily a how-to book, I reveal all the tricks that I know to

---

2. I am not alone in detesting that vile, Gollum-like creature. As lawyers Dahlia Lithwick and Brandt Goldstein wrote in *Me v. Everybody: Absurd Contracts for an Absurd World* (Workman Publishing, 2003): "3. The Maniacal-Paper-Clip-With-Eyebrows Provision. You will delete/disable/destroy whatever it is that allows that inane little bastard to leap around the bottom right-hand corner of my screen, emitting what can only be described as a mechanical fart and incessantly observing: 'I see that you're writing a ransom note …' or assuming that I wish it to turn all my letters into spreadsheets and my correspondence into numbered lists."

mitigate the most awful effects of bad program design—for example, turning off the confirmation dialog ("Are you sure? Really sure? Really, really, really sure?") that appears when you send a document to the Windows Recycle Bin. More importantly, this book explains what you and I need to do to make our voices heard in the software industry so that it stops sucking, hopefully soon. It worked for Clippy, didn't it?

At the same time, I have to tell you that developing software is different in many ways from developing physical objects, things that you can drop on your foot. When you build, say, a table out of wood, the inherent properties of the material preclude some design choices and dictate others. For example, you know that you can't weld it, but you can fasten it with screws, and you can make it only so thin before it bends unacceptably. Software, on the other hand, imposes very few inherent constraints. It is almost infinitely tractable. As Frederick Brooks said in his classic book on software development, *The Mythical Man-Month* (Addison Wesley, 1995)—which I've suggested that he retitle to *The Mystical Geek-Week*, because of today's accelerated project schedules—programmers work with "nearly pure thought-stuff." I've always described programming as trying to stuff smoke into a bottle. So I'll explain to you what really is inherently difficult to make a program do (surviving a power blip, for example, or making a new program compatible with previous versions[3]) as opposed to what's simply a boneheaded design decision by an idiot designer who should have known better.

I teach software development at Harvard University Extension School and at companies all over the world. I've written nine books for programmers and development managers, along with many journal articles and newsletters. Despite these disadvantages, I promise you that my writing is never dry. I did my best to stay away

---

3. A favorite programmer joke runs, "How did God manage to create the world in only six days? He didn't have any installed base he had to worry about backwards compatibility with." My editor points out that He also skimped on documentation.

from geek jargon. For example, you won't find the word *gigabyte* appearing in this book,[4] but I'll refer to "a quarter's worth of disk space," which is about the same thing at the time of this writing.

I've found this book surprisingly easy to write compared to some of my others. The late sportswriter, Red Smith (1906–1982), liked to say, "Writing is easy. You just open your veins and bleed." As I hope you've already seen, I feel passionately about the issues I raise here. When I finish ranting in a live talk ("Windows XP is a decent product for the price. Windows 98 is an inferior piece of crap that isn't worth the powder to blow it to hell"), my students often say, "Gosh, Platt, stop beating around the bush and tell us how you really feel." To which I reply, "If you're accusing me of calling 'em as I see 'em, I plead guilty as charged." This book is not just an explanation for you; it's my cry to the heavens for sanity in this crazy profession. And I hope when you read this, you'll add your voice to mine.

---

4. Yes, I know, except for this once, wiseguy.

1
· · ·
WHO'RE YOU CALLING A DUMMY?

"That'll never sell," I sneered at the title in the bookstore. "Who would publicly buy a book that proclaimed to all the world that he's a dummy? It'd be like buying condoms labeled 'extra small.' "

We all know how that one turned out, don't we? *DOS for Dummies* and its companion, *Windows for Dummies*, became the best-selling computer books of all time. The concept has spread to fields far beyond computing, with titles as disparate as *Wine for Dummies*, *Saltwater Aquariums for Dummies*, and *Breast Cancer for Dummies*. The series has sold more than 100 million copies, according to *Getting Your Book Published for Dummies*, which I bought to help me find a publisher for the volume you are now reading.[1]

Computers make users feel dumb. Literate, educated people can't make that infuriating beige box do what they want it to do, and instead of marching on Microsoft with torches and pitchforks and hanging Bill Gates in effigy, they blame themselves and say, "Gee, I

---

1. Sometimes this approach backfires. In October 2003, the U.S. Consumer Product Safety Commission recalled the book *Candle & Soap Making for Dummies* because incorrect instructions for mixing certain chemicals could create a burn hazard. I'm not sure what that implies for the publisher's breast cancer book, or its stablemate, *Prostate Cancer for Dummies*.

must be dumb." In a society where nothing is ever the fault of the person doing it, where people sue a restaurant when they spill their own coffee, getting users to blame themselves for anything is a magnificent accomplishment, albeit probably not the main one the software vendor intended. Why do programmers design applications that make people feel this way, and why do people meekly accept this abuse from their computers?

WHERE WE CAME FROM

The designers of the earliest computer programs didn't care about making their products easy to use. Solving the computing problem at hand—for example, dealing with a printer to make the words come out properly on paper—was so difficult that no one had time or money left over for making a user's life easier. A computer's thinking time was enormously expensive, much more so than the user's time. Forcing the human user to memorize complicated commands instead of using computer power to provide a menu listing them made economic sense. The relative costs are now reversed, but almost everyone in the industry older than about 30 grew up in that type of environment. It can't help but shape our thinking today, no matter how hard we try to leave it behind. Think of your older relatives who grew up in the Great Depression of the 1930s, who even today can't bear to throw away a sock with only one hole in it.

Like driving a car in the early years of the twentieth century, early users expected computers to be a pain in the butt, and we were rarely disappointed. Almost all users were programmers themselves. Few of them felt the need, or often even the desire, to make things easier. We accepted the difficulties—the rationed computer time, the arcane commands, the awful documentation—as those motoring pioneers accepted hand-cranked engines and constant tire punctures. It was the best anyone had. We were happy to get our important computing jobs (tabulating the census, cracking enemy codes) done at all, as they were happy to stop shoveling horse manure out of the barn every day. We liked fiddling with our programs, using them in ways their designers never intended, as the early motorists liked tinkering with their engines. If someone had told Henry Ford that his Model T needed a cup holder, he'd have laughed in that person's face.

There was a feeling in those days that making programs easy to use was just plain wrong. If a program was hard to write, it *should* be hard to use so that only those who had proven themselves worthy through intellectual struggle could benefit from the programmer's effort. I remember, with surprising fondness even today, the pride I felt on discovering that the command to print a document on the first major computer system I ever used (1975, freshman year in college) wasn't Print or P, but rather, the letter Q, since you were placing the document in a queue to be printed. I had learned a magic word. I was becoming one of the elect. I was Smart!

But as hardware got cheaper, and computers moved from the air-conditioned glass rooms attended by high priests to the workbenches of geeky hobbyists and then to the desktops of individual employees and the homes of real people, they had to become easier to use. So the developers of applications had to start putting time and money into designing a program that users could actually use. Why hasn't it worked?

WHY IT STILL SUCKS TODAY

The piece of a computer program that deals with the human user— getting commands and input data from him, displaying messages and output data to him—is known as the **user interface.** As with many areas of computing, user interface design is a highly specialized skill, of which most programmers know nothing. They became programmers because they're good at communicating with a microprocessor, the silicon chip at the heart of the machine. But the user interface, by definition, exists to communicate with an entirely different piece of hardware and software: a live human being. It should not surprise anyone that the skill of talking with the logical, error-free, stupid chip is completely different from the skill of talking with the irrational, error-prone, intelligent human. But the guy who's good at the former is automatically assumed to be good at the latter. He's usually not, and he almost never realizes that he's not. That's what causes programmers' user interface designs to suck, at least from the standpoint of the poor schmoe that's stuck using that piece of junk.

How does this happen? Programmers have to have a certain level of intelligence in order to program. Most of them are pretty good at dealing with the silicon chip; otherwise, they get fired very quickly and encouraged to take up another profession in which they might possibly benefit society, such as roofing. How can they turn into lobotomized morons when designing a user interface? For one simple reason, the same reason behind every communication failure in the universe: They don't know their users.

Every programmer thinks he knows exactly what users want. After all, he uses a computer all day, every day, so he ought to know. He says to himself, "If I design a user interface that I like, the users will love it." *Wrong!* Unless he's writing programs for the use of burned-out computer geeks, his user is not him. I tell my programming students to engrave on their hearts, along with the phrases "Garbage In, Garbage Out" and "Always Cut the Cards," Platt's First, Last, and Only Law of User Interface Design:

Know Thy User, for He Is Not Thee

To take the simplest example, consider a personal finance program, such as Quicken or Microsoft Money. These get used for a few hours every couple of weeks. A user won't—can't—remember as much of the program's operation from the previous session as she would for an application she used every day. She will therefore need more prompting and guidance, which an all-day every-day user (such as the programmer) finds intrusive and annoying. It's impossible for a programmer to put himself into the shoes of such a user. The programmer knows too much about the program and can't conceive of anyone who doesn't.

Because they're laboring under the misconception that their users are like them, programmers make two main mistakes when they design user interfaces. They value control more than ease of use, concentrating on making complex things possible instead of making simple things simple. And they expect users to learn and understand the internal workings of their programs, instead of the other way around. I've done them both, and I now repent the error of my foolish younger ways.

CONTROL VERSUS EASE OF USE

Every time I teach a class at a company, I ask how many of the students drive cars with a manual, stick-shift transmission (as I do). Usually about half the students raise their hands. I then ask how many more *would* drive stick shifts if their wives would let them, or if they came on the minivans that they need to drive because they're turning into old-fart curmudgeons like me. Usually about half the remaining students raise their hands.[2] "Now, would you not agree," I ask, "that a stick shift takes more work to learn and to use than an automatic, but gives somewhat better control and performance if you do it right?" They know they're being led somewhere they don't want to go, but they can't usually wriggle out at this point, so they agree suspiciously. "Now, what percentage of cars do you think are sold with stick shifts in the U.S.?" They squirm uncomfortably and say something like, "I bet it's low; 30 percent?" They wish. Sales estimates vary from about

---

2. Try this test around your company. It'll tell you something about your user population that you might not have known. Then use this book's Web site (www.whysoftwaresucks.com) to tell me the results you get. Thank you.

10 percent to 14 percent. Let's call it 12.5 percent, or one out of eight, for easy comparison.

This means that six out of eight programmer geeks value a slight increase in control and performance so highly that when they spend $25,000 or more on Motor City iron, they're willing to do more work continuously over the life of the product to get it. But only one out of eight of the general population makes the same decision when offered the same choice. And it's actually much lower than that, because all six of those geeks are in that one out of eight. The percentage of normal people willing to tolerate the extra effort is almost zero. Programmers value control. Users value ease of use. Your user is not you.

Here's an example of doing it wrong. AT&T directory assistance was once simple and easy. You'd ask for someone's number and the automatic voice would say, "The number you requested is 555-1212. Please make a note of it." If you stayed on the line, it'd repeat the number so that you could be sure you'd written it down correctly. Simple. Easy. Impossible to screw up. Good. Then AT&T added the capability of automatically dialing the number for you. They'd say, "The number you requested, 555-1212, can be automatically dialed for an extra charge of 50 cents. Press 1 to accept and 2 to decline." The simple thing was as easy as ever, and the newer, more powerful feature was available to those who wanted it enough to pay for it. Anyone who didn't like the new feature could simply hang up. Then some idoit [*sic*, see note[3]] had an absolutely awful idea. The last time I tried AT&T directory assistance, it said, "The number you requested

---

3. This word comes from a class I once taught. A particular student didn't do well because he didn't work very hard, and he would write me these long, impassioned e-mails about how unfair it all was. On the one hand, he was obviously quite upset. On the other hand, it's difficult to take someone seriously who is allegedly in the final year of a college education and has not yet learned the proper spelling of the word *idiot*. He would write, "Platt, you're an idoit. And the grader is an idoit, and the guy who recommended this class is an idoit, and I'm an idoit for listening to him." Ever since then, my staff and I have used the word *idoit*, pronounced ID-*oyt* (or *eed-WAH* if you're French), to designate someone so clueless that he doesn't even know how to spell *idiot*.

can be automatically dialed for an extra charge of 50 cents. Press 1 to accept and 2 to decline." It wouldn't give me the number until I entered my choice. I had to take the phone away from my ear, visually reacquire the keypad (which gets harder after age 45 or so), put down the pencil I was holding in my other hand to write down the number, press the correct button, pick up the pencil again, and put the phone back to my ear. Only then would it tell me that the number was 555-1212. The complex, powerful operation is possible, but the simple operation is no longer simple. The designer of this system clearly valued control over ease of use, but I guarantee that his users don't. Whoever inflicted this on the world should be forced to do it 500 times every day. He'd shoot himself by the end of a week.

My cell carrier, Verizon, on the other hand, has taken ease of use to new heights. Verizon realized that almost everyone calls directory assistance because she wants to phone someone immediately, so why not just do it? When I dial directory assistance from my cell phone, the automated voice says, "The number is 555-1212. I'll connect you now." It happens automatically, without any motion or even thought on my part. The new number stays on my phone's recently dialed list so that I can add it to my contact book if I want to. The few callers who only want to write the number down can simply hang up, which they'd be doing then anyway. Simple things are simple. Complex, powerful things are simple, too. This design is as good as AT&T's is bad.[4]

I DON'T CARE HOW YOUR PROGRAM WORKS

The second mistake programmers make when they design user interfaces is to force users to understand the internal workings of their programs. Instead of the programmer adjusting her user interface to

---

4. I just read today that Verizon is planning to offer driving directions to the location of the phone whose number you ask for, locating your phone by its embedded GPS chip. I sure hope they do it in a way that doesn't break the simplicity and power they already have.

the user's thought processes she forces the user to adjust to hers. Furthermore, she'll usually see nothing wrong with that approach. "That's how my program works," she'll say, puzzled that anyone would even ask why her user interface works the way it does.

Here's an example of what I mean. Open Windows Notepad, or any other type of editor program, and type in any random text. Now select File, Exit from the main menu, or click on the X box in the upper right of the title bar. You'll see the message box shown in Figure 1–1.

What exactly is this box asking us? It seems to be saying that some file changed, but I haven't seen any file anywhere. What the hell does "save the changes" mean?

The answer is that Notepad usually edits documents (called files by computer geeks) which live on your computer's hard drive. When you open a document, Notepad copies it from the disk into the computer's memory. As you add or remove text by typing, the program changes the contents of this memory copy. (In this example, we didn't open an existing document, but the program created a new one in memory, giving it the name "Untitled".) When you're finished working on the document, the program has to write the memory copy back to the disk, an operation called **saving the file**. Otherwise, the work you've done will disappear, and you'll get very angry.

The programmer wrote the program this way (copy the document from disk to memory, make changes on the memory copy, and write it back to disk) because that was easiest for her. And it's not a bad way to write a program. Reading or writing characters from the

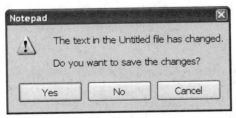

FIGURE 1-1 Notepad asking the user whether to save changes

disk (spinning iron platters with moveable parts) is roughly a thousand times slower than doing it in memory (electrons moving at the speed of light), so this probably *is* the best way for this simple program to work internally.

But the programmer's user interface exposes these workings directly. How can that be bad? She's forcing you to understand that she's written the program this way. You shouldn't have to know or care about her program's internal workings to use it successfully, as you shouldn't have to know or care whether your car's engine uses fuel injection or a carburetor in order to drive it.

You don't normally think in the way that this program works. Most people think of editing a computer document as analogous to the paper-and-pencil (remember those?) method. You make marks with the pencil and there they are on the paper. You erase the ones you don't want. If you don't want any of them, you crumple up the paper and throw it away. The work you've done is permanent, unless you expend energy to get rid of it. But that's not the choice Notepad gives you. Every single new user of computers gets caught on this — selecting No, in which case Notepad discards the work you've done, which hopefully isn't much. Eventually, the user learns to think like a computer program, or more precisely, like the programmer who wrote this mess. User interface design guru Alan Cooper defines a "computer-literate user" as one who has been hurt so many times that the scar tissue is thick enough so he no longer feels the pain.

The question and its answer would be much clearer if the message box asked "Throw away everything you've just done?" It's exactly the same question, just asked from the user's point of view rather than the programmer's. But the programmer is thinking only of her program's operation, writing to the disk, and asks you whether to do that. She's requiring you to wear her shoes; she hasn't even tried to put herself in yours. If she had, she'd ask the question a different way. She might then see the ridiculousness of asking it at all, and design a better user interface, even if the underlying program worked the same way.

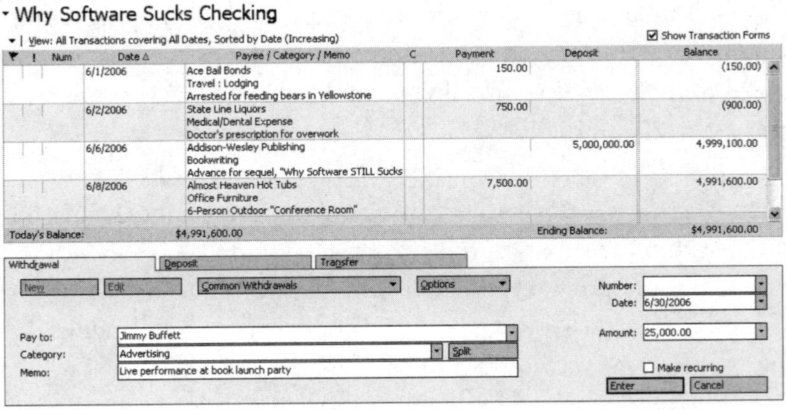

▾ Why Software Sucks Checking

	!	Num	Date △	Payee / Category / Memo	C	Payment	Deposit	Balance

▾ | View: All Transactions covering All Dates, Sorted by Date (Increasing)   ☑ Show Transaction Forms

			6/1/2006	Ace Bail Bonds Travel : Lodging Arrested for feeding bears in Yellowstone		150.00		(150.00)
			6/2/2006	State Line Liquors Medical/Dental Expense Doctor's prescription for overwork		750.00		(900.00)
			6/6/2006	Addison-Wesley Publishing Bookwriting Advance for sequel, "Why Software STILL Sucks"			5,000,000.00	4,999,100.00
			6/8/2006	Almost Heaven Hot Tubs Office Furniture 6-Person Outdoor "Conference Room"		7,500.00		4,991,600.00

Today's Balance: $4,991,600.00   Ending Balance: $4,991,600.00

Withdrawal	Deposit	Transfer

New   Edit   Common Withdrawals ▾   Options ▾   Number: [ ] ▾
     Date: 6/30/2006 ▾

Pay to: Jimmy Buffett   Amount: 25,000.00 ▾
Category: Advertising ▾   Split
Memo: Live performance at book launch party   ☐ Make recurring
     Enter   Cancel

FIGURE 1-2 Microsoft Money user interface, looking like a checkbook

Microsoft Money, the personal finance program, does a better job. Its designers understand that the user's mental model is a checkbook, and his screen looks like a checkbook register (Figure 1–2). It feels familiar and comfortable (well, relatively) to a new user. The check that you're currently working on is shown in a different color. You enter the check's details and press Enter. The check moves up, changes color to look like the rest of them, and a new empty check appears in the work area. If you have sound turned on, you hear a "ka-ching" cash-register type of sound.[5] The program doesn't ask you whether to save the check. The act of pressing Enter tells the program that you want to keep that information. If you later change your mind and want to change the data on a check or delete one entirely, you click on that check in the register and type in the new information. When does the program read its data from the disk to memory, and when does it write it back again? I don't know and I don't care. And I don't want to and neither do you. The program's user interface

---

5. The sound itself is an anachronism. When was the last time you actually heard that sound from a cash register? The registers in modern stores beep and whir like the computers they are. But we still have the sound, as we still talk about dialing phone numbers, when most of us haven't touched a rotary instrument in decades.

follows your mental model, instead of forcing you to learn and deal with the internal design choices of its programmers.

That's a much better way of designing a user interface. As a user, I don't want to think about the program itself. I want to think about the job the program is doing for me—for example, do I have enough money to pay this bill? Another user interface design guru, Donald Norman, expressed this feeling very well in the title of one of his books: *The Invisible Computer* (MIT Press, 1999). Ideally, I wouldn't think about the program at all.

That's one major reason programs are hard to use and make you feel dumb. You're being forced to think like a programmer, even though you're not one and you don't want to be one. You shouldn't have to. You don't have to think like a mechanic to drive a car, you don't have to think like a doctor to take an aspirin, and you don't have to think like a butcher to grill a hamburger. You're paying your hard-earned money for this product. It's the programmer's job to adjust to you, not the other way around.

A BAD FEATURE AND A GOOD ONE

Here's another way programmers screw up user interfaces and make their users feel dumb. On your Windows desktop, select a document, any document. Then press the Delete key. Unless you've figured out how to disable that feature, you'll see a confirmation dialog box like the one in Figure 1–3, asking whether you really want to delete the file.

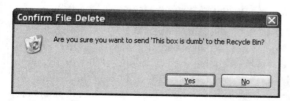

FIGURE 1-3 Useless confirmation box from Windows Recycle Bin

Have you ever, even once, said, "Whoa! I didn't want to do that. Thanks for asking me," and clicked No? Have you seen anyone do that, or even heard of that happening? I haven't. Confirmation has been so vastly overused that it has, ironically, become completely useless. Because this box is constantly "crying wolf," like the shepherd boy in Aesop's fable, no one pays attention to it, even when it's warning you of a file you really don't want to delete. You've seen it so often that it doesn't register. You cruise through it on autopilot, clicking Yes unconsciously. It provides you with no safety whatsoever. None. Fortunately, you can turn off this particular confirmation dialog.[6] Many others exist that you can't get rid of, and none of them should exist. At all. Anywhere. Ever.

Other operations in life don't require confirmation. Your car does not ask, "Do you really want to start the engine?" when you turn the key. The supermarket clerk does not ask, "Do you really want to buy these?" when you place your groceries on the register belt. Think how many more books you've bought from Amazon.com since you discovered their patented 1-Click ordering capability.[7]

Why do programmers constantly ask for confirmation? They do it because they think their users are confused and don't understand the consequences of what they've just told the program to do. That may well be true, given the awful quality of the rest of the user interface. But confirmation doesn't solve this problem. If the user was confused when he first gave whatever command triggered the confirmation box, he'll be even more confused when he sees it. Since the program seems reluctant to do what he told it to do, he

---

6. Right-click on the Recycle Bin, select Properties from the pop-up menu, and uncheck the "Display delete confirmation dialog" checkbox.

7. It's a little-known fact that, in the earliest prototype of this feature, Amazon's programmers actually did pop up a confirmation dialog box saying, "Are you sure you want to order this with one click?" when the user clicked the 1-Click order button, thus making it a two-click process. They fought viciously to keep this feature, and required a direct order from Amazon's president, Jeff Bezos, to remove it and make it truly a one-click process.

thinks he's made some kind of mistake. The use of a confirmation box keeps programmers from having to a) clearly explain to the user what he's doing, so he doesn't try to do stuff he doesn't want to, and b) provide a way to recover in the event the user really does do something that he later regrets.

But what if the user really is making a mistake? If you put, say, a flashlight on the register belt with a package of the wrong size batteries, wouldn't an attentive clerk ask, "Are you sure you want these?" Shouldn't a good user interface save us from mistakes like that? It certainly should, and one of the beauties of computer programs is that it can. But that won't happen by blindly asking, every single time, "Are you sure you *really* want to do whatever the hell it is that you just told me to do?" Instead, a good user interface would prevent the problem from ever occurring in the first place. Perhaps the Web page selling flashlights would contain a checkbox saying, "Include batteries." It'd be checked by default, because the flashlight won't work without batteries. A buyer who already has lots of batteries in that size could uncheck it. Or better still, the flashlight would be shrink-wrapped with batteries already inside it, so it would work the instant you unwrapped it and no one would ever have to think about it. A smart user interface designer would have thought of that before programming even started. If a programmer thinks he needs a confirmation box, I guarantee you that he's screwed up some other part of the user interface that would prevent the need for it. He probably hasn't even tried, and it probably never occurred to him that he should. Confirmation is a crutch for the lazy or ignorant programmer, paid for by every user. And it's one that doesn't work.

But wouldn't you want to confirm destructive acts, such as deleting the file? No, not really. Another reason you aren't asked to confirm starting your car or buying those groceries is that these operations are easy and cheap to undo if you suddenly realize you've made a mistake. You just turn off the ignition or return the unwanted item. Computer programs can very quickly and easily make copies of documents and pieces of memory. This allows programmers to provide users with the ability of reversing actions they've performed. This Undo capability is one of the very best in the user interface designer's arsenal. To my mind, it's the single biggest advance in user interface design since the mouse.

If you click Yes on the confirmation box in Figure 1–3 (or if you've turned off the box completely), Windows doesn't actually wipe the document off your computer. Instead, it moves it to another area of the disk, called the Recycle Bin, which is analogous to the famous trash can on the Macintosh. If you change your mind after doing this and want the document back again, you can retrieve it from the Recycle Bin as long as you haven't emptied the bin. You really do want to move the file almost all of the time. It's much more efficient to fix the relatively small number of errors that actually do occur (for example, a slip of the mouse that caused you to select the wrong file for deletion; I did that yesterday) than attempt to prevent them by annoying every user with a confirmation box at every deletion, especially since the latter doesn't work because of its overuse. An ounce of cure is not worth five pounds of prevention.

The Undo feature can work not only with file operations, but also within applications. It's usually found on the Edit menu, along with its companion, Redo (which undoes the undo, of course). I can't write for five minutes without undoing something; typing a foolish sentence, perhaps, or moving text to the wrong place. The programmers who implement this feature are any user's best friends. I buy them beer whenever I meet with them, and so should you. It takes an enormous amount of effort to make this feature work so that users don't have to think about it ("Easy is hard," the saying goes); just Ctrl-Z (little and ring fingers of the left hand) and back it all comes. A program should confirm only the operations that it can't undo. And it should be able to undo everything.

The real beauty of Undo is that it allows users to explore a program. It's not always easy to understand a new program's operation from the short labels on menu items and the tiny pictures on toolbar buttons. But because Undo exists, a user can experiment by trying different things, knowing that he won't damage something that can't be repaired with a few keystrokes. I can move a paragraph around to see how I like it somewhere else, and quickly undo the operation if I don't. Programmers often regard incorrect user input as the act of an idoit who should have sat down and read the manual. It isn't. It is the primary mechanism by which the human species learns. An application with Undo capability becomes explorable, not frightening. It recognizes and enhances the user's humanity. Failure to implement it properly is a mortal sin.

If Undo is implemented correctly, there is only one destructive operation in the entire system, and that's emptying the Recycle Bin. Some would say that this operation should have a confirmation dialog box, as it currently does. But even here, the confirmation dialog exists only to guard against another bad design, placing the Explore context menu item right next to Empty Recycle Bin. One slip of the mouse, sliding down three spaces on the context menu rather than two, and you get the latter rather than the former. Bad. Since it's the only destructive action in the system, emptying the Recycle Bin should have a special action used for no other purpose, maybe clicking both mouse buttons on it at once (an operation called **chording**), or clicking on it while holding down some key. Better still the Recycle Bin should empty itself automatically, deleting files after they've been inside it for some configurable amount of time, maybe starting at a month, so that you rarely have to empty it manually. Don't you wish your home garbage cans would do that? You should never see a confirmation dialog anywhere, under any circumstances. A programmer who shows one has abdicated responsibility and should not be in the user interface business.

STOPPING THE PROCEEDINGS WITH IDIOCY

Programmer-designed user interfaces are at their absolute worst when communicating error messages to the user. Just today while goofing off from writing this chapter, I read CNN.com's home page and wanted to save a copy of it to my disk. I selected File, Save from my Web browser's menu. A dialog box appeared showing the progress of the saving operation—5% complete, 15% complete, and so on, up to 99% complete. Then that box went away and up popped the one in Figure 1–4.

This box is the creation of a true idoit. Why couldn't the Web page be saved, and is there anything I can do to fix it? Was the page copy protected somehow, as professional artist sites sometimes try? Was the server unavailable? Why did the progress bar get up to 99 percent if the operation was failing? Where's the 99 percent of the page that it told me it saved? That's not as good as 100 percent, but I'd much rather have it than nothing. Why has it disappeared? The box says the page couldn't be saved to the selected location; does that mean it could be saved to some other location? If so, where, and how would I know? If not, why is it mentioning location? The browser has already successfully shown me the page, that's why I said to save it; why doesn't it just save the data it's actually showing? The box doesn't tell me how to figure out exactly what the problem is, or where to go for more information. And for a response, it offers only the OK button. No, it is *not* OK with me that this operation didn't work and the program can't explain why. Even the title of the box, "Error Saving Web Page," is erroneous. I didn't make an error. I did what the program allowed me to do. The program made an error when it wouldn't save my page and then made another when it couldn't explain why. To cause all this confusion with only 15 words, two of which are *the*, is the greatest accomplishment of idoicy I've ever seen.

FIGURE 1-4 Really stupid dialog box

Alan Cooper, the user interface design guru I mentioned previously, refers to situations of this type as "stopping the proceedings with idiocy," an excellent phrase even if he doesn't use my spelling of the last word. If I really can't save that page, my browser should know that, prevent me from trying, and somehow explain it to me, ideally without popping another stupid box into my face. Perhaps the Save menu should be grayed out when I go to that page, maybe changed to read "Can't Save–Protected" so that I'd know what and why. If it can't save the entire page, it should save what it can and inform me about what it missed—again, without making me click on another stupid dialog box. Perhaps the saved page would include placeholders in the areas it couldn't save, showing the little red X graphic used in the browser display when a requested page element can't be found.

By rooting around behind the scenes, I was able to piece together what happened. I had set my browser to block certain types of annoying content. The browser displays them as blank areas on the screen, which I vastly prefer to the stupid dancing advertisements that usually appear there. (I'll discuss the idoicy of dancing advertisements in another chapter.) When the saving portion of the program encountered these portions of the page and found them blocked, it didn't ignore them as the display portion of the program did. Instead, it choked on them, aborted the entire process instead of keeping what it could, and stopped the proceedings with the idiocy I just described.

How can anyone not feel like a dummy when someone pops up an incomprehensible box like that? By knowing that it's not your fault at all, but rather that the programmer is failing in his duty. By realizing that no user should have to understand such a stupid communication. By imagining your hands around that programmer's throat and your knee slamming into his crotch like a pile driver. By following the suggestions at the end of this chapter and in the last chapter of this book.

TESTING ON LIVE ANIMALS

A programmer would never ship a product without testing its internal operation (OK, she *shouldn't*). Why would she think she could get away without testing a user interface, to find out whether users really can use it? Because she knows she likes it and finds it usable, so how could anyone else fail to do so? As we've already seen, this unconscious assumption is almost always wrong. Computers that users can't figure out how to use are very expensive paperweights. Testing the user interface, called **usability testing,** is difficult and expensive, but necessary.

She can't just give users her program and ask them afterward how they liked it. They often won't remember what they did, or they won't want to tell her about a problem they had because they feel stupid that they couldn't figure it out, or they won't want to insult her by telling her what a complete pile of crap the product of her last two years of professional life has turned out to be. (This is a problem that I do not have, as you've probably guessed by now.) To find out what works, programmers have to observe exactly what users do in the act of dealing with the user interface. What do they try to do first? Where do they go next? How many times do they try something before they actually figure it out? How long does it take them to notice such-and-such a feature?

And they have to observe in a manner that doesn't affect the users' behavior. This means the users have to be in an isolated room, having access to only whatever support materials (e.g., online documentation, or maybe Google) they will have in real life. You have to watch them through one-way glass, videotaping their reactions, and have logging software so that you can see exactly which keystrokes and mouse clicks they used to try to deal with your application. Some usability labs even have tracking headsets that report which part of the screen the user is looking at.

When you do this, the light bulb goes on. As Alan Cooper wrote in his classic book, *About Face: The Essentials of User Interface Design* (IDG Books, 1995): "[Usability professionals] drag programmers into dark rooms, where they watch through one-way mirrors as hapless users struggle with their software. At first, the programmers suspect that the test subject has brain damage. Finally, after much painful observation, the programmers are forced to bow to empirical evidence. They admit that their user interface design needs work, and they vow to fix it."

Unfortunately, usability testing often gets left until late in the development process, just before the product ships. Schedules invariably slip,[8] so usability testing is often omitted completely. When it actually does turn up useful information, the schedule often doesn't allow time for changing the program in response. Usability testing needs to be done early, ideally before any programming takes place.

Some companies think that vast amounts of testing just before release will result in a more usable product. For example, Microsoft does what it calls "dog-fooding," which is short for "eating our own dog food." Just before the company releases a product to the public, it'll give it to real users inside the company—for example, switching the secretaries over to the next edition of Word for Windows. This does catch some bugs, by which I mean programmer logic errors, where they forgot to carry the two or something, causing the program to break. But that's too late for catching design errors, particularly in the area of usability. Eating your own dog food before releasing it to users helps your dog food taste slightly better than it otherwise would. But it won't change it into cat food, and the dog food stage is too late to discover that your users really are cats, or giraffes.

Here's an example of doing it right. I once consulted at an insurance company that was writing a Windows program to replace some expensive IBM terminals. Unusually for an insurance company, they actually did the usability testing that I just told you about. And they did it properly, too, with videotape and programmers

---

8. In one of my books for programmers, I coined Platt's Law of Exponential Estimation Explosion, which simply states: "Every software project takes three times as long as your best estimate, even if you apply this law to it."

watching through one-way glass. They found that the users basically liked the application and found it usable. But the users had the habit of pressing the Enter key to move from one input field to the next, as their IBM terminals did, rather than the Tab key, as Windows applications do. Couldn't the developers change that, they asked? After thinking it through carefully, the developers decided that, although it would be quite easy technically, it wouldn't make the users happy, even though the users thought it would. Sure, they could make this application work the old way. But all the new commercial Windows applications the users were soon going to have wouldn't work that way, and the users would soon go schizoid switching back and forth many times per day. So the developers convinced the users to bite the bullet and make the change. And after the requisite period of squawking, the users calmed down and swallowed it, helped by the abysmal job market in the area at that time. My point is not that programmers should cram down users' throats the features they think would be good for them. You usually can't get away with that; this was a special case. I'm relating the story to show you how a client of mine did a good job of usability testing. They did the testing they needed to do. They found what there was to find. And then they made the right decision based on what they found. I wish more companies would do that.

WHERE WE ARE AND WHAT YOU CAN DO

Where does that leave us poor users? To summarize my points so far:

1. You *are not* dumb. User interfaces really do suck, and they shouldn't.
2. They suck because they're designed by programmers, who don't realize that their users aren't like themselves.
3. Because of point 2, their interfaces are intentionally complex, and they expect you to like dealing with that, which you don't (see point 1).

User interfaces could be made much better by involving usability specialists from the beginning of every software project. General programmers are worse than useless in this regard. Someone has to speak for the silent majority of users who don't give a flying fish about the technology for its own sake, who just want to get their work done so that they can get back to living their lives. I try to fill this role at every design review I attend. "You're like the guys who design the drills that they sell at Home Depot," I tell the programmers. "Here you are, arguing over this or that internal detail of drills, ball bearings versus roller bearings versus air bearings, each of you claiming that's what your customer wants more than anything in the world. Wrong. The customer doesn't care about your drill for its own sake, not one tiny bit. Never has, never will. He doesn't go to Home Depot because he wants a drill. He goes to Home Depot because he wants holes. If he could just buy a box of holes to put on his wall, without having to touch a drill, he'd be much happier. (Remember Ringo in the movie *Yellow Submarine?* "I've got a hole in my pocket...".) Your drill is a necessary evil in your user's quest for holes. Now ask yourself, and answer truthfully: "What kind of hole does your user really want, and how is your program going to get him better holes, faster, for less money?"

Now that you've finished this chapter, you're as qualified as anyone to tell software vendors what you like and what you don't like. The structure of a program's user interface was not handed down as a commandment on Mount Sinai. It's created by the design decisions of programmers and other developers, who could just as easily make other ones. Send them e-mail, lots of it. Tell them what you like and what you don't like. Tell them to get that confirmation thing out of your face and provide better Undo capability.

More than anything else in the world, programmers hate looking dumb. Ugly, impotent, unkind to children and small animals, they don't care, but dumb? May the Good Lord have mercy on us. Their view of themselves prizes intelligence far above everything else. If you need to make a programmer do something, ensure that he'll look stupid in public if he doesn't do it.

So the next time you see a badly designed user interface, stop and look at it. Play for a while; figure out exactly and specifically why you don't like it, and what would make you happier. Post a notice about the bad design on a "Hall of Shame" Web site that exists for this purpose. This book's Web site, www.whysoftware-sucks.com, would be a good place to start. Then send e-mail to the application company, showing them your public exposé. The more stupid you've caught them being, the more it'll gall them to see it publicized. Then they might, *might* finally get it through their heads that their users aren't themselves.

2
. . .

TANGLED IN THE WEB

The World Wide Web is big. (Annoyed Reader: "I paid you how much to tell me that?" Royalty Counting Author: "What? You mean it's not?") From connecting a few dozen academic physicists, the Web has mushroomed into what one author calls "the backbone of the human race." Browsing the Web is primarily why you have a PC today, and it's moving to your TV, your cell phone, and even your refrigerator.[1]

But the Web falls short of its potential because so many programmers and designers that create and run Web sites don't understand what it's for, how it works, and what it does, even though they should and they claim to. Every user has a bad Web story or ten, as they also have a bad desktop software story. You spent half an hour entering information on multiple pages, and then got a "Too busy, try again later" message on the final submission and lost all your work. Or the browser froze and never showed any response, and you didn't know whether you'd successfully bought those Bruce Springsteen

---

1. The LG GR-D267DTU Internet Refrigerator comes with an automatic ice maker, a built-in touch screen PC, and a connector for a high-speed Internet connection. I've never actually used one, but reviews indicate that it integrates well with the same company's Internet microwave, air conditioner, and clothes washer.

tickets. And you worry constantly about bad guys creeping through the Internet wire into your very bedroom to steal your money or identity. This chapter discusses the difficulty that users have in figuring out and using Web sites, as the first chapter did for desktop software. Later chapters will talk about the security and privacy of both.

People often use the terms World Wide Web and Internet interchangeably, but they really mean completely different things. The Internet is a general-purpose data network that carries any type of data from any intelligent box in the world to any other intelligent box in the world. The World Wide Web is a specific type of data that travels over the Internet containing pages that a human reads in a browser such as Internet Explorer or Firefox. The construction of the World Wide Web on top of the Internet is a mighty tale. Let's see if I can tell it in only four nontechnical paragraphs.

WHERE WE CAME FROM

The World Wide Web originated at CERN, a large academic physics laboratory in Geneva, Switzerland. Scientists there placed their research documents on networked computers to save paper and shelf space, and users read them with an early browser program that ran on their high-powered, expensive workstations. Then in 1990, a guy named Tim Berners-Lee said, "I see that documents often refer to other documents. Since they're all online already, wouldn't it be great if the reader could jump to a referenced document with a single click? We'll call it, hmmm, let's see, how about a 'link'?" The document creators agreed on the text characters that would designate a link and specify its target, modified the browser program to detect a click on it, and thus the Web was born. But it wasn't worldwide yet.

Since the research documents often referred to documents at other labs, the next problem was to connect CERN's document system to those at the other labs. It was a relatively simple matter to make the document systems talk to each other over the Internet, the general-purpose network that already connected them and was used at the time primarily for e-mail. Users could now jump back and forth between documents without caring or even knowing where a document physically lived. And thus the Web became worldwide. But it wasn't all that popular yet.

The Web really took off around 1994, a year in which the number of Web servers went from 500 at the beginning to 10,000 by the end. This happened partly because of an improved browser program called Mosaic, which later evolved into Netscape Navigator, developed, again, at an academic physics lab. This was the first good (OK, half-decent) browser for cheaper platforms such as Windows, which was just then becoming ubiquitous in the home and workplace. Colleges and businesses that already used the Internet for e-mail started placing their documents on it and browsing the documents placed by others, and home users started doing the same with their telephone modems. This started a virtuous cycle, in which more users attracted more content, and more content attracted more users. And thus the Web took off.

The academics who started the Web don't like this, but the main forces driving the Web's phenomenal growth are the prime motivation for essentially all (nonacademic) human activity: money and sex; often combined. The Web makes it much easier for a customer to find and retrieve any type of data—text, music, pictures, anything; from anywhere. Sometimes the owner of that data charges money for the data itself. Pornographers made this business model really sing, as few users will fork over the bucks for any other type of Web content, even today. A few businesses, notably the *Wall Street Journal* (porn for a different audience, some would say) and the *Oxford English Dictionary*, are enjoying limited success with this model, and mainstream music companies may eventually figure it out if they ever get their heads screwed on straight. More often today, the owner of the data makes money by using the Internet's easy access to that data to lower the friction of existing business processes, such as removing human employees from airline reservation systems or package delivery tracking. And thus the Web became ubiquitous.

HOW IT WORKS

The Web was originally designed to deliver static pages containing text and, sometimes, pictures. By static I mean that a human being creates them in advance of a user's request for them, sitting down with a word processor and writing them out like newspaper or magazine articles. When a user requests a Web page by typing its address into her browser or clicking a link, the server that owns the page reads the page from its disk and sends it to the user. The server doesn't do any thinking about the user's request; it simply finds and returns the article that the human author had previously written, as shown in Figure 2–1.

The Web used in this way represents human-to-human communication. Think of the pages as paper brochures and the Web as a very fast postal service without the machine guns. You can do an awful lot with this simple architecture. For example, my local art cinema has a small Web site that I sometimes browse to see what's playing (such as *Happy, Texas,* in which two escaped convicts are mistaken for beauty pageant organizers in a small Texas town), read about coming attractions, and follow links to trailers and reviews. The cinema doesn't have to spend money and kill trees to print and snail-mail me their paper brochures, and I don't have to remember

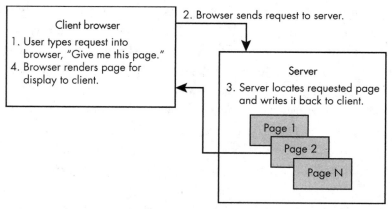

FIGURE 2-1 World Wide Web, human-to-human communication

where I put the darn thing or worry that my wife has thrown it out. For another example, when's the last time you saw a printed computer manual? Storing them online costs the company much less than printing them on paper, and having users download them is far cheaper than paying postage. And users don't have to wait for delivery, it's easier to update them for new releases, and it's easy to keep older ones available for customers who need them. Serious computer geeks used to complain that they couldn't read the online manuals in bed, but wireless connections have pretty well solved that problem (though not the marital problems caused by reading computer manuals in bed, unless two geeks are married to each other).

Many, many kinds of documents benefit from this approach. Commuter train schedules that change a few times per year. Newspapers and magazines. Employee and student handbooks. Company annual reports. Brochures for vacation resorts, museums, and attractions. Reams of government regulations. Even more reams of pornography. Functioning as a faster and cheaper postal service is arguably the Web's greatest success to date.

But humans, as always, are greedy. The circuit in your brain that says "More!" doesn't have any sort of modulating input. Regardless of the cool stuff you manage to acquire, after about five minutes you automatically say, "Yeah, great. More please. And hurry up." While browsing their static documents, users thought to themselves, "If I can see this physics report or that movie listing on my screen rather than on paper, why can't I see my bank statement? And why can't that picture of a belly dancer shimmy enticingly?"

Although they look the same to a user, these new requests present a different and much harder computing problem to the programmer. A bank can't create a new page every day for every possible view of every account, as a newspaper does for every article. There are far too many accounts and too many different ways of viewing them—sort by check number, payee, or amount; sort in ascending or descending order; show the last 30, 90, or 120 days; and so on. Instead, the bank's Web server gets input from the user;

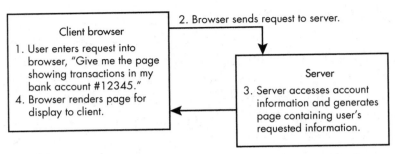

FIGURE 2-2 World Wide Web, human-to-computer communication

in this case, the account number and the way he'd like it sorted. The bank's server then looks up the account in a database and creates, on demand, a Web page detailing the account, as shown in Figure 2–2.

Instead of human-to-human, we're now doing human-to-computer communication. This is an entirely different activity. There are, or were, many human jobs which consisted of talking to a human customer on the phone, typing the customer's request into a computer, and reading the answer from the computer's screen back to the customer over the phone. Tracking a FedEx package, buying an airline ticket, and moving money from one bank account to another are transactions of this type. We call these **human touch points,** and they're incredibly expensive. A financial industry client once told me it cost his company about $25 for a human operator to handle an account transfer request, and 10 cents if the customer did it himself online.[2] "And when you do 5 million of them a day, that difference adds up real quick," he said. When you call FedEx on the

---

2. That sounds incredibly high for an operator who earns maybe $10 per hour, but the costs add up faster than you think. You have to pay benefits, such as insurance. You have to train the person. You have to train someone else for when she goes on vacation or gets run over by a bus (see insurance). You have to hire a supervisor and send him to sexual harassment sensitivity class with periodic refreshers (see insurance). You need a human resources department to track and document that this has been done. You have to rent a building for them all to sit in, and pay the electric and phone bills. And so on.

phone and track a package by talking to a human operator, FedEx's shareholders are sorry you sent that package because they lost money on the deal. The discount airlines that are making money today, or at least losing it more slowly than the legacy carriers, are the ones that sell the highest percentage of their tickets on their cheap Web sites instead of involving expensive human reservation operators. There's a lot of money here for businesses that are sharp enough to pick it up.

And they do have to be sharp. Because, as I said, this dynamic case is a much harder computing problem. Often the data they access is private, which means the server has to verify the user's identity (called **authentication**, see Chapter 4) and decide whether he's authorized to see the data he's asking for. You want to see your bank account balance, but you don't want your angry ex-wife looking at it, do you? The server has to remember what a user was doing from one page request to the next so that the airline ticket payment software can know the correct fare to charge you based on your route selections. The server and your browser have to encrypt sensitive data on the network wire so that your neighbor's geeky teenage son can't read it with a packet sniffer. And the server has to do all of this correctly, within the three or so seconds that you are willing to wait before saying, "The heck with it" and picking up the phone or going to their competitor's site.

WHY IT STILL SUCKS TODAY

Users, of course, don't know how hard the computing problems are that the site has to solve, and they wouldn't give a flying fish if they did. They only care about the part that they see, the site's public face, the user interface. Web site user interfaces fail to do their jobs for the same reason a PC program user interface fails: The Web designers don't know their users, and thus they think that by extension, they must be like themselves. They're not, the designers don't realize that they're not, and the results show it. Because designing a Web site looks easy, people who have no business touching it (managers, marketers) think they can design a good one: "I know what users need because I am one." That's like saying that undergoing a root canal qualifies you to perform one.[3] If programmers are bad user interface designers, these amateurs are even worse. And there's no excuse for it. It takes no more work to design a good Web site than it does a bad one. But it does take smarter work, and that's much harder to find than it ought to be.

Web design guru Vincent Flanders once wrote on his Web site[4] that the number-one cause of bad Web design is "believing people care about you and your web site." He's entirely correct. I tell my students, "Your user doesn't care about you. Never has, never will. Your mother might, if she can stand to look at your site for more than a few seconds, but no one else does." Unless a designer is constructing a site for his mother (and many family sites are indeed designed with this in mind), he needs to get it through his head that a user hasn't come to his site to make him happy. And even a mother looking for pictures of her grandchildren isn't going to tolerate a bad Web site design for long.

A user comes to a Web site because she needs or wants something for herself. She probably wants to a) find some useful information for her day-to-day life, such as train schedules or driving directions or a package's current location; b) shop for a product or service, such as books or music or travel, or darned near anything on Earth from eBay; or c) be entertained, generally by people wearing very little clothing.

Web designers often make the same mistakes as designers of desktop applications: making complex things possible instead of making

---

3. Former U.S. Supreme Court Justice Sandra Day O'Connor, in her autobiography, *Lazy B* (Modern Library, 2005), describes a cowhand on her family's ranch doing this to himself. She does not describe him quitting the cowboy business and opening a dental practice.

4. www.webpagesthatsuck.com

simple things simple, and requiring the user to understand their internal workings instead of adjusting their interfaces to the user's thought processes. The designers get so wrapped up in putting in all the bells and whistles they can think of, just because they can, that they forget that users aren't interested in the process at all; they're interested only in getting the results they want with the absolute minimum of effort. If a user could click her heels and say a magic word to renew her library books or track a package, she'd do it, instead of firing up her PC and dealing with a Web site.

In addition to these classic errors, Web site designers face two major challenges that desktop software designers don't. The first is that viewing a Web site is a very casual interaction, much more so than installing a program on your PC. Essentially every user first arrives at a Web site from a search engine, or sometimes by typing in an address or clicking a link they found in an advertisement somewhere. They initially don't know what the Web site can do for them. The Web site's home page needs to visually explain this in the first two or three seconds they'll spend there before they say "Screw it" and go to the next link in their search engine list. Later in this chapter, I'll show you an example of a site that does this well and one that does it poorly.

The second problem is site navigation. A desktop program usually has a command menu and toolbar at the top of the application's window, and users know to look there for a list of commands. The commands are more or less standardized as well: File, Edit, Help, and so on. But when you're viewing a Web site, the menu and toolbar belong to the browser (Back, History, Stop, etc.), so navigating and giving commands to the Web site (go to the flight search page, then find airline flights from Baltimore to St Louis on Thursday) has to be done in some other way. The site's navigation structure (which places can I go to on this site, how do I get there, which one will solve the problem I came here to solve) needs to be obvious to the user within a two- or three-second glance, and too few of them are. I'll show you good and bad examples of this, too.

Above all, a good Web site minimizes the amount of work a user has to do, particularly work that deals with the site itself, rather than the task the user came to the site to accomplish. An excellent Web design book by Steve Krug shouts this philosophy from its title: *Don't Make Me Think* (New Riders Publishing, 2000). Here's an example of how one Web design team followed that advice and another one ignored it. You tell me which Web site you'd rather use.

CLIENT-CENTERED DESIGN VERSUS SERVER-CENTERED DESIGN

The World Wide Web is, by definition, worldwide (stop me if I get too technical here). A user in, say, Sweden, can access Google just as easily as a user in the U.S. can. Google has therefore translated its home page into many languages, from Afrikaans to Zulu, often through the services of volunteer translators.[5] When a user in Sweden types www.google.com into her browser, Google's server detects that her request came from Sweden, makes the stunningly brilliant deduction that she therefore probably speaks Swedish, and automatically sends her Google's Swedish home page (see Figure 2–3).

Besides offering Google's services in Swedish, you can see that this page contains a direct link to Google's English home page, in case the person accessing Google from Sweden doesn't speak Swedish, or a Swedish speaker wants to practice her English, or Google erred in detecting the country from which the request came. All of Google's other languages are two clicks away using the Språkverktyg link, or three clicks away if the user goes

---

5. I find it amazing that a huge, highly profitable company such as Google manages to attract unpaid volunteers to do its work, but somehow it does. The volunteers must figure that Google would never spend its own money to translate its site into their native languages, such as Burmese (14 percent complete at the time of this writing, according to Google.com), Sanskrit (68 percent), and Klingon (96 percent).

FIGURE 2-3 Google.com home page in Swedish

first to the English page in which the same link is labeled Language Tools. If the user does switch languages, Google automatically remembers that preference on her computer (with a Web cookie, explained in Chapter 5) and shows her that language's home page the next time, regardless of where the request comes from. (Malaysian and Thai guest workers in Sweden find this feature handy.) The language choice is correct for almost all users almost all the time, with exactly zero thought and effort, and it takes only one (usually) to three (maximum) clicks to fix it permanently if it's ever wrong. This type of automation improves everyone's Web experience, often without the user noticing, which is really good design. I give it the highest accolade a reviewer can: "It just works."

How does Google know which country the user's request is coming from? Every Web page request automatically includes what's called the **Internet Protocol (IP) address,** the network identifier of the user's computer. Think of it as caller ID for Web page requests.[6] Just as for telephone number country codes, these addresses are assigned to Internet providers by a central regulatory body. As it's easy to look up a telephone number's country code to find the country in which a phone resides, so it is easy to look up an IP address to discover which Internet provider owns it and the country in which it resides. The server can then send the page in the correct language for that location. The home page for a multilingual country (Canada, Belgium, Switzerland) can offer the user a choice the first time and then remember it, or get even fancier with its response based on the location — perhaps requests originating in the Canadian province of Quebec would first appear in French and those from British Columbia would first appear in English.

I've written a sample page for this book's Web site (www.whysoftwaresucks.com) that demonstrates this technique for detecting a user's country. It took me less than half an hour to get this page working, so it's not very hard to do, although bringing it up to industrial strength would take a little longer.

So then why the *hell* doesn't UPS.com do something similar? I hope you're sitting down when you see how much harder UPS makes people's lives. According to its Web site, United Parcel Service delivers 14 million packages per day, 90 percent of them in the U.S. UPS.com gets 145 million hits per day, an average of about ten per package. Users can track packages and schedule pickups without needing to talk to a human. UPS benefits greatly from hiring fewer human operators, as I discussed earlier in this chapter.

Since UPS delivers to every address on the planet, it makes sense that it should have a Web site for Swedish users, and it does

---

6. As I discuss in Chapter 5, it's not difficult to defeat this technique if you want your surfing to be ultra-private, as it's not difficult to block caller ID from displaying your phone number.

(see Figure 2–4). But getting to it is nowhere near as easy as getting to Google's Swedish page. If you simply type www.ups.com into your browser, from Sweden or anywhere else, you see the page in Figure 2–5, which requires you to select your location manually. UPS.com doesn't automatically detect it as Google does, and it won't talk to you at all until you tell it your country, which Google will. To get UPS.com's Swedish page, you have to click the country selection box to open it, type S to jump to that letter in the list, then click the down arrow 26 times to reach Sweden (a lot of countries begin with S), click the list to close it, and then click the

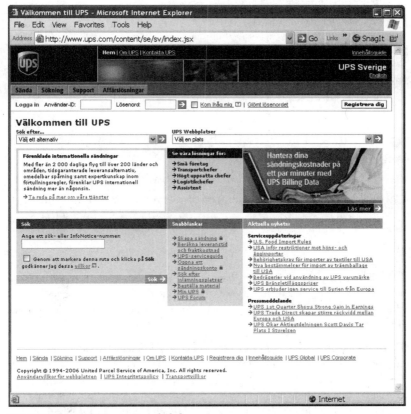

FIGURE 2-4 UPS.com Swedish home page

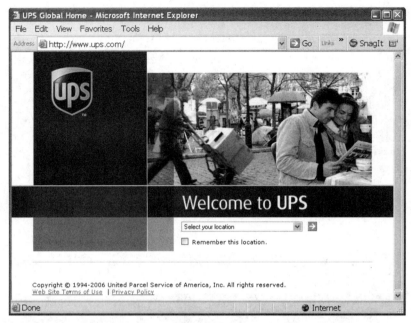

FIGURE 2-5 UPS.com global home page

forward arrow to go there. Only then will it show you the UPS Web page for Sweden.[7, 8]

This isn't a very nice way to greet Swedish visitors, now, is it? Thirty user interface clicks before you can even *start* doing the work you came here to do, as opposed to zero with Google? That's not

---

7. A serious geek pointed out to me that a careful Swedish user could type T to jump to Tadjikistan, then click the up arrow three times to reach Sweden. Suggesting that users navigate to Sweden via Tadjikistan is the exact opposite of the design strategy "Don't make me think."

8. Another careful Swedish user might try typing W immediately after the S, trying to jump to SWeden, which often works in a smart program such as Outlook. Unfortunately, the country list in UPS.com is too dumb to do that. It interprets the W not as the second character of a word, but rather as a new first initial, and takes you to the country of Wallis and Futuna (a French territory in the South Pacific between Fiji and Samoa, even farther from Sweden than Tajikistan).

how a company gets people to use its cheap Web site instead of call-ing its expensive human operators. And UPS isn't wasting the time of only Swedish users, either. Users from the United States, who account for 90 percent of UPS packages sent, need at least four mouse clicks to select their country. Simply showing the U.S. page by default would eliminate this step for 90 percent of all users, and would leave the others no worse off.

We wouldn't accept this guff from a human user. Suppose you walked into a regular post office building to send a package. What would you do if the clerk said, "First, click this button 30 times to tell me which language you want me to speak." At the very least, you'd say, "Well, doofus, in case you were too stupid to realize it, we're standing in [whatever country] and I greeted you in [whatever language]; why not at least *try* that one and see how far you get, as soon as I stop strangling you?" Why do we meekly accept this sort of abuse from computers? We don't have to, and we shouldn't.

UPS's Web programmers could not possibly know enough programming to develop a site that handles 145 million hits per day without being aware of the possibility of deducing a user's country from the incoming IP address. They therefore must have deliber-ately chosen not to do so. They might have foolishly intended to provide control at the cost of ease of use, as we saw in the previous chapter: "Hey, what a *cool* feature! You can access *any* country's site, no matter where you are! Let's give it to *everybody!*" Possibly they fell into the old geek mindset of wanting any errors to be the user's fault. But if one in ten of those 145 million hits goes to the country selection page, and if selecting the country takes an aver-age of five seconds, UPS.com wastes an entire human lifetime on this foolishness every single month. It didn't value the time of its users. It probably never occurred to UPS that it should.

UPS.com developers will point out that you can tell their site to remember the correct country page by checking the "Remember this location" box on the front page, or you can bookmark your desired country page in your browser. The latter takes up precious bookmark real estate for something you might use only occasionally. The former requires you to make a decision about saving the country before you see the page your selection takes you to, which no one wants to do. Worst of all, both approaches make you think about and deal with the site infrastructure itself rather than the work you came to the site to do. That's no way to make a good first impression on a new customer. And it's even worse for users in Switzerland (32 to 34 clicks, depending on the language you select) and Syria (35 clicks). If the inhabitants of the latter country ever turn their bile from editorial cartoons to Web usability, I'm afraid that UPS is in some really deep doo-doo.

UPS guys, listen to your Uncle Plattski. Google does it well. You do it poorly. Google provides an excellent default choice. You provide none at all. If the user selects a language other than the default, Google remembers it automatically. You insist on explicit user action to remember it. You are treating your customers with contempt, the people who put bread into the mouths of your children and a roof over their heads. I know you don't care because you're geeks with no social skills (a redundant description if ever there was one). But because that's what you are, I know what will bother you far more: Your design choices make you look stupid compared to other programmers. Users, mere *users*, are laughing at you now that I've shown them how dumb you are *choosing* to be. If I were you, I'd fix it.

WHERE'S MY EYE OPENER?

I wrote in the preceding chapter about programmers' need for control, their tendency to make complex things possible rather than making simple things simple. They often require the user to understand and adjust to their internal programming model rather than adjusting their programming to the user's thought processes. Here's a Web site that does it right and one that does it wrong.

FedEx Kinko's, the copy-store chain, has more than a thousand stores in the U.S. One of the main reasons a customer visits its Web site is to find the store nearest him. Kinko's Web designers have made finding this information about as easy as it could possibly be. Their home page (see Figure 2–6) asks a user to type in the ZIP Code (bottom row of the picture, just left of center; it shows up better in color in the browser) near which he wants a store. The result page (Figure 2–7) shows the five nearest stores, along with their contact information, the services available at each, a map showing their locations, and a link for driving directions to the one you select. Answering the simplest question, "Where is the nearest store?", is very simple to do, and answering more complex questions, such as whether that store has the services I need and how do I get there,

FIGURE 2-6 FedEx Kinko's home page showing simple locator

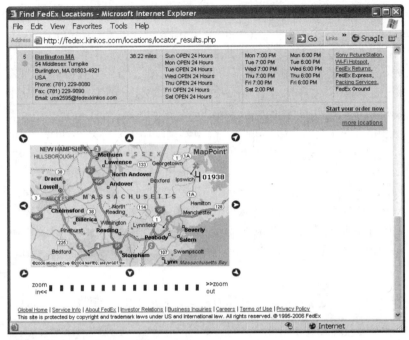

FIGURE 2-7 Kinko's store locator response page

happens automatically while answering the simple question. This is as well as I've seen this sort of thing done, and about as well as I can imagine it being done.

Contrast this with Starbucks.com, the Web site of the famous coffee roaster. This site also has a store locator, but you have to leave the home page to reach it. When I go to that page (see Figure 2–8) and type in my own ZIP Code of 01938, the result page says (in a tiny font, even though I have my browser font on its largest setting), "No stores were found in the proximity range you selected. Increasing your search to a larger proximity may return stores in your area. Would you like to search again?" (See Figure 2–9.)

What the hell is going on? I don't recall selecting a "proximity range." I just typed in my ZIP Code. Did the control labeled Search Radius have something to do with proximity ranges, whatever they

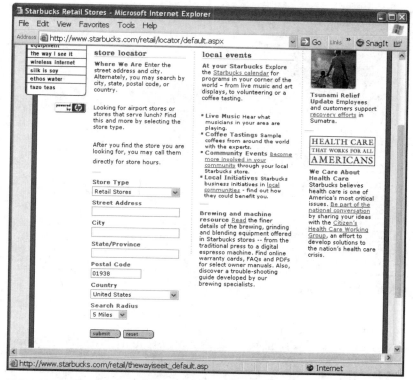

FIGURE 2-8 Starbucks.com store locator page with search radius control

are? If so, why doesn't it use the same term, and if not, what the hell is it talking about? Why is it in a font I can't read, even though I have my browser set to one that I can read? More importantly, why do I have to think about this nonsense at all? I haven't had my coffee yet this morning; that's why I went to Starbucks.com to find the damn store. I asked it the simplest of questions and it expects me to decode four-syllable words to understand why it won't answer, and to fiddle with controls to fix it. Why won't it just tell me where the nearest store is located? To hell with this idiocy,[9] I'll have a cup of tea. And a Valium. I think I need one.

---

9. See Chapter 1 for the definition of the term *idoit*.

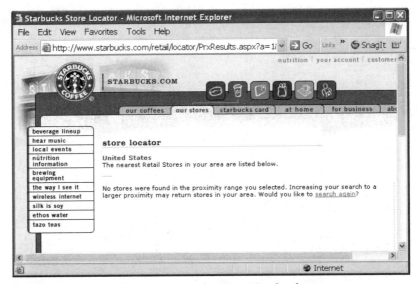

FIGURE 2-9 Starbucks.com saying there's no Starbucks store near me

Starbucks' Web programmers have made the mistake of exposing their internal programming logic and forcing the user to adjust to it. Behind the scenes, both Kinko's and Starbucks' Web servers get their geographical data from another Web server called MapPoint, as shown in Figure 2–10. MapPoint knows the locations of these and many other types of businesses, it knows how to find the businesses near a specified location, and it knows how to generate maps and driving directions. I've worked with MapPoint in this type of application. I know that when you do a search of this type, MapPoint requires a limit on the distance to search, from one to 100 miles. This makes sense from MapPoint's internal programming standpoint, because finding every Starbucks in the entire U.S. requires more computing work than it wants to do, and users care only about the nearest one or two locations anyway. It turns out that's the purpose of the Search Radius control at the bottom of the Starbucks store locator page: It specifies the distance within which you want MapPoint to search. Kinko's automatically figures out

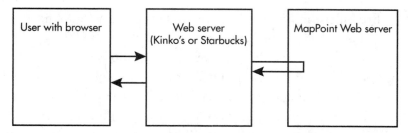

1. User sends own location to Kinko's or Starbucks site, asking for nearby stores
2. Web site asks MapPoint for store locations and maps
3. Web site takes information from MapPoint, formats it into a Web page that looks nice to the user
4. Web site returns page containing nearby stores to user

FIGURE 2-10 Kinko's and Starbucks Web sites using MapPoint service to find location of store

what that radius should be and supplies it to MapPoint internally, without bothering the user,[10] but Starbucks makes the user think about it and breaks if the user gets it wrong.

The Starbucks programmers probably think that having more control over the search is powerful and cool. But in reality it's a useless and annoying distraction. Nobody goes around asking, "Is there a Starbucks within five miles? How about ten? Fifteen?" But many people ask themselves, many times a day, "Hey, I'm thirsty and I need a jolt, and I don't mind paying $2.50 for a shot of espresso that costs 15 cents to make. Where's the nearest Starbucks?"[11] The Kinko's user interface design understands and respects the user's thought process, whereas Starbucks' does not. If Starbucks wants to

---

10. What value does Kinko's use and how do they calculate it? I don't know and I don't care. And I don't want to, and neither do you. I just want my damn coffee. Hey, Starbucks, stop asking me stupid questions and just tell me where it is, OK?

11. As Tim Hartford writes in *The Undercover Economist* (Oxford University Press, 2006), "By charging wildly different prices for products that have largely the same cost, Starbucks is able to smoke out customers who are less sensitive about price. Starbucks doesn't have a way to identify lavish customers perfectly, so it invites them to hang themselves with a choice of luxurious ropes."

try a five-mile search radius first (and in fairness, that does find 166 stores when asked for the New York City ZIP Code of 10021), fine, but it should do so internally without any user input, automatically enlarge its search if it doesn't find any stores, and not come back to the user until it's done its best. Then if it *still* hasn't found any stores, it should commiserate with the user, perhaps with a page saying something like "You poor bastard. There's no Starbucks for 100 miles. Click here to go to our mail order department and we'll FedEx your fix by tomorrow morning. (Their stores are easy to find, even if ours aren't.) Or click here to go to our franchise center and learn about opening your VERY OWN Starbucks store. Sure looks like you need one. Just don't drink up all the profits." Probably the Starbucks programmers, hyper-caffeinated even by programmer standards, can't imagine that any place on Earth could possibly be more than five miles from a Starbucks store. (How many times do I have to say it? Your. User. Is. Not. You.)

Imagine the following letter to Jim Donald, president of Starbucks: "Dear Jim, I had to use the store locator on your Web site three separate times to locate my nearest Starbucks store because it's 11 miles away. The right number would have been once. How hard do I have to bang my head against the wall to get you to take my money? Why don't you make it easy for me the way Kinko's does? Tell your Web designer to buy a copy of *Why Software Sucks* and read it, provided they know how. Meanwhile, I'm going to your archrival, Peet's Coffee."

IT'S OBVIOUS—NOT!

When a user gets to a Web site, the site's functions and capabilities need to be obvious. The user has to immediately see what the site can do for her, and what she has to do to make it do that. The world's best example of that is Google (see Figure 2–11), probably the most recognized site on the entire Web. The user sees it, understands it, *gets* it, immediately. It's clean and simple, without any

FIGURE 2-11 Google's English home page, as short and sweet as they get

spinning, animated logos so beloved by marketingbozos (see Chapter 6) to "build our brand awareness." The complex, seldom-used or experimental features such as text messaging are accessible through the "more>>" link without distracting users of its most fundamental operations. It's so easy to understand that you could practically figure it out from the Swedish page shown previously in Figure 2–3. I have a hard time seeing any way to improve it.

Contrast this with Coke.com, shown in Figure 2–12. What can anyone do at this site? Something, I guess, or it wouldn't be here, but what? I can't tell. The legends "The Coca-Cola Company," "Coca-Cola Worldwide," and "Coca-Cola In the USA" tell me exactly zero. I have no idea what the buttons do until I move my mouse over them, a technique that Vincent Flanders calls "mystery meat navigation." Even if I follow the USA legend (Figure 2–13), I *still* don't know what the site does for me. The navigation links are all over the screen—top, bottom, left, right, a few in the center. Except for the

FIGURE 2-12 Coke.com home page. What does it do? I can't tell. Something, I guess, or it wouldn't be here.

FIGURE 2-13 Coke USA page. I still can't tell what it does or why I should come here.

"TV ads" link, I can't imagine from looking at them what any of them do, and I pity anyone who feels the lack of TV ads so strongly that he spends his life searching for more. Is there free music here, deals on soda, sponsorship for my worthy cause, nutritional information (ha!), anything about the Olympics that Coke spends so much money on sponsoring? Not that I can see. There's no search box or obvious link to one, so I can't find what I want that way. It's not clear to me why this site exists in any way, shape, form, or manner.

Contrast this with Coke's archrival, Pepsi.com (see Figure 2–14). A user can see all kinds of stuff on the very first page. Music. Sports. Promotions. A false-rumor alert. Nutrition information, cell phone ring tones, movie tie-ins. A search box in case whatever I'm looking for

FIGURE 2-14 I can see what this page can do for me. I might not want any of it, but at least I can see it.

isn't obvious. An earlier version offered the chance to win Super Bowl tickets for life. I know what this site can do for me and where to start looking for it. It's a far better design. It has its own problems which I'll discuss later, but at least the home page shows the kinds of things that you can do on the site.

Vincent Flanders figures that the Coke people are confusing Web design with sex. He writes on his Web site, "In the real world, foreplay is mandatory. You have to set the mood, you have to be gentle, you have to entice. Fine. But in the world of the web there's no place for foreplay. It's not necessary. It gets in the way. To put it bluntly, the web is 'Wham. Bam. Thank you Ma'am.' People don't need to be enticed or put in the mood when they visit your site. They're there for a particular reason and the sooner you give them what they came looking for, the better."

Google knows that. I come to the Google site to search for other sites, and it gives them to me extremely well, with zero fuss. Coke fiddles and diddles and never does get to the point, if indeed it has one. Pepsi does it far better, except for one thing. You can't see it in this book, but the center picture on the Pepsi site spins around in a way that makes me quite dizzy. It is to that annoyance that we will now turn our attention.

SPLASH, FLASH, AND ANIMATION

Two of the worst techniques in any Web designer's arsenal are splash pages and animation. A **splash page** is a home page that doesn't do anything except say, "You found our site." The useful work that a site can accomplish, the "real" home page, is accessed through a link from the splash page. The Coke page shown in Figure 2–12 is a good example. Splash pages waste a user's time. How many people would ever use Google if typing Google.com into their browser bar led to a page saying, "Hi, thank you for coming to Google. Aren't we cool? Now click here to go to the page that will actually allow you to search." No site should have one. Anywhere. Ever.

Animation, likewise, is vastly overused. It usually requires a piece of software called Macromedia Flash Player that plugs into your browser, although other techniques are sometimes used. According to one former Macromedia employee, Flash was originally designed to serve up animated porn—the shimmying belly dancer I referred to earlier. My editor won't let me develop that idea any further, but I'm sure you can imagine it just fine. Besides that excellent and worthy use, a few Web design scenarios exist in which video is perfect for accomplishing whatever the user has come to the site to do. The classic example is furniture manufacturer Ikea, which uses it to show the assembly of its furniture far more clearly than printed instructions ever could. Excellent. Fabulous. Wonderful. God bless the Web.

But far more often, designers throw in motion all over the place, just for the sake of doing so. Many Web page advertisements use this technique because the human eye is naturally drawn to motion. In the screenshot from Slate.com (see Figure 2–15), the Dell banner at the top, the cell phone on the right, and the AT&T logo balls at the bottom are all dancing around while I'm trying to read the article. I don't want my newspaper jumping around when I read it. It's especially bad when I haven't had my coffee (refer to the Starbucks store locator fiasco earlier in this chapter). This annoying overuse of motion causes users to remove all motion capabilities from their browsers, missing the good as well as the bad. Fortunately, products are available that allow you to easily turn animation on and off at will. Many ad blockers do so, and so do dedicated products like Flashblock from mozdev.org and No! Flash from Baryon Lee.

As bad as splash pages and gratuitous animation are on their own, the combination of a Flash/splash page makes users scream to the heavens at its awfulness. Reviewer Julia Lipman, in an Internet newsletter titled "digitalmass.com," describes "scores of rococo splash pages that do little except showcase their designer's capacity for self-indulgence." User interface design expert Jared Spool says in a Web column that "When we have clients who are thinking about

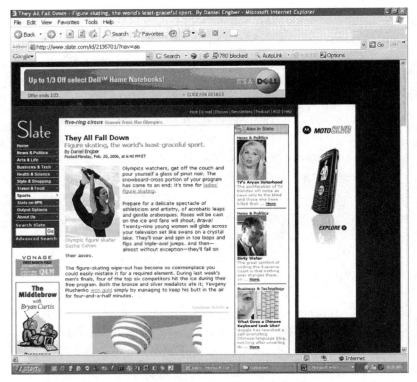

FIGURE 2-15 Three dancing ads on the same page. Who can read the articles with all that going on?

Flash splash pages, we tell them to go to their local supermarket and bring a mime with them. Have the mime stand in front of the supermarket, and, as each customer tries to enter, do a little show that lasts two minutes, welcoming them to the supermarket and trying to explain the bread is on aisle six and milk is on sale today. Then stand back and count how many people watch the mime, how many people get past the mime as quickly as possible, and how many people punch the mime out."

The most annoying one I've yet seen is at HowardSystems.com (see Figure 2–16). It runs for about a minute, with captions moving left and right, and you can't do any work until it's finished, unless you

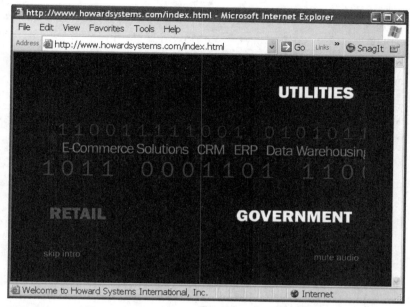

FIGURE 2-16 HowardSystems.com Flash splash page. This is the worst I have ever seen in my life and a classic example of flashturbation.

click the faint "skip intro" link. You can't even enter the site by clicking on the center of it, which is what most users would try first. The term *Flashturbation* was coined to describe just this type of site. The company clearly spent a lot of money on it, and someone in high management looked at it and said, "Hey, great! Put it up there, people will love it." What kind of drugs was that guy on? What kind of drugs was his mother on when she was pregnant? And what, after all the time-wasting annoyance, is the slogan of this foolishness? "You have a job that needs to get done NOW!" Damn right I do, so shut up, stop jumping around, and get the hell out of my way so that I can do it.

TESTING ON LIVE ANIMALS

A Web site needs to be tested on its actual users, just as a PC application does, and it's not hard to do. All you need is a video camera, some user bait such as free beer, and some patience. You give users a specific task to accomplish, watch them try to do it, and see how and where they fail. As Jared Spool likes to say, "We just follow the money and look for the pain."

Believe it or not, it's sometimes hard to get designers to test a user interface at all. As reviewer "inhollywood" wrote in an Amazon.com review of Spool's book:

> I had a recent experience with a designer who was invited to observe users of a large commercial real estate she had designed. She declined, saying 'I have no need to know what people think of the design. I designed it with a specific purpose in mind, and I believe I achieved my goal. What could I learn?'
>
> What arrogance! Well, guess what folks? The users testing the site found it confusing, hard to navigate, difficult to search, and therefore not something they'd be likely to use. I guess if her purpose was to drive people to better sites, she succeeded.

Even when they recognize the need for testing, designers often don't do it well. They test their designs on themselves, or on people who work on their team. To nobody's surprise, it passes with flying colors ("We can all use it just fine, so we must have gotten it right. Good job, guys."), but it crashes in flames when real users try it. The designers of the site already know why the site exists and the sorts of things it can do, and therefore can't begin to imagine how it appears to anyone who doesn't. Yet explaining itself to new visitors within a few seconds is the number-one problem a site design has to solve, because if it can't do that, no one will look at the rest of it. The designers already know how to navigate the site, so they can't test whether the navigation system is clear to a user who doesn't. They already know the way their site requires the user to enter data, such as leaving out the spaces from credit card numbers, so they can't tell whether a new user can figure it out. And so on.

Site designers often don't know which tasks to give their testing users. I've heard them say "Tell us what you like and don't like about the site" rather than something a real user would come to the site to do—say, "buy an air ticket to Tallahassee with the lowest fare for July." Jared Spool writes of a test he once did for Ikea.com. Ikea's designers had told their test users to "find a bookcase." Not surprisingly, all the users typed "bookcase" into the site's search box and found them quickly. But when Spool told the users, "You have 200+ books in your fiction collection, currently in boxes strewn around your living room. Find a way to organize them," the users behaved very differently. They browsed the site's aisles instead of using the search box, and the few times they did search, it wasn't for the term "bookcase," it was for "shelves." The users had a much harder time because their mental model was very different from that of the site designers. The designers wouldn't have realized that, if they hadn't been smart enough to do the testing and have a third party ask unfamiliar questions.

Sometimes a Web page sucks like a vacuum cleaner for reasons that are obvious to users but not to corporate marketing idoits. For example, Spool's testing found that the animated logo on one Disney site was so annoying that "Users first tried to scroll the animation off the page, and when they couldn't, actually covered it up with their hands so they could read the rest of the text." I would have paid money—in fact, would *still* pay money—to see them show that video to the president of Disney. He'd probably tie the site designer into a straitjacket and make him ride "It's a Small World After All" for two solid days before allowing him to drown himself.

WHAT YOU CAN DO ABOUT IT

Web sites exist to serve their users. You can see now that good Web design is possible and at least occasionally does happen. When it doesn't, it's because designers don't understand their users, even though they should. In my experience, most Web site designers really do want to do a good job and make a good site. So tell them. Most sites provide a link for sending feedback to the site owner. They are often more appreciative than you would think of good feedback; the more specific the better, especially if you can point to the functionality you are requesting as already existing somewhere else on the Web.

For example, I recently used the feedback link on Alaskaair.com to send them the following note: "You list flights from Boston to Seattle only in order of price. I chose your airline specifically because you have the only nonstops on this route, and I have trouble picking them out of the much longer list containing all the connecting flights. Other travel sites, such as Orbitz, allow me to limit the choice to nonstops, or at least show them separately so that I can see them clearly. I'm finding yours harder to use than theirs, making me more inclined to pick up the phone and talk to your expensive human reservation staff. I hope this helps you make your site more useful. Quickly."

A few months after I sent that, the site improved, as shown in Figure 2–17. It now contains a radio button control allowing the user to sort the flights by number of stops, departure or arrival time, or price. They did an even better job than I suggested by adding other sorting options with easy access. Certainly many customers will want to sort flights by the lowest fare, and others will want the first or last flight in or out on their travel days.

I don't know whether Alaska Airlines did this because of my note or despite it, or whether they even read it. But if you don't tell a company what you want in its site, don't be surprised when you don't get it. And of course, sometimes you won't get it no matter what you say. Sometimes you want the exact opposite of what ten other people want. And sometimes the site owner just ignores you. Although I sent feedback to both Starbucks and UPS, neither of them has done anything about the problems I describe in this chapter. I have a funny feeling this book will get their attention.

Sometimes a site owner doesn't seem to want feedback. Again, UPS.com is the best, or worst, example. You have to work your way

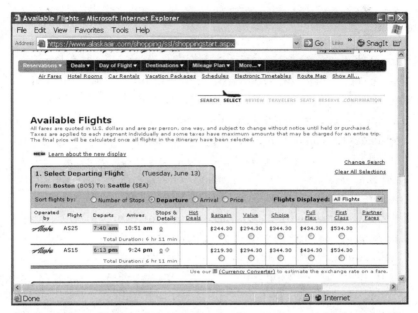

FIGURE 2-17 Alaska Airlines' Web site showing improved functionality after feedback

down through five separate screens with cryptic names to reach the feedback form,[12] and then fill out seven separate sections before they'll allow you to submit it. (I'll put a link on this book's Web site to make the process easier, so you can bombard them.)

Being polite never hurts, though I sometimes have trouble restraining myself from screaming at the worst errors, especially when they waste my time by losing my work. And I envision 100 nasty e-mails per day arriving at UPS.com from Sweden, all beginning with, "Yøur site sücks, yøu dumb åsses." The site designers

---

12. Go to www.ups.com and select your country. Then select the very small Contact UPS link at the bottom of the page. Then select Internet Technical Support, and then Contact Internet Technical Support, which for some reason is so different from Internet Technical Support that it needs its own page. Then select Email UPS Internet Technical Support. Then fill out the form and click Submit. Ever get the feeling they really don't want to hear from you?

don't know why they suck or they wouldn't have done it that sucky way. Just shouting "You suck!" doesn't usually accomplish much, even if it's true, especially if it's true.

Except, of course, when it's done publicly, by a recognized authority on a site with a lot of traffic. "Hall of Shame" sites exist for this specific purpose, but the granddaddy of them all is WebPagesThatSuck.com, run by Vincent Flanders, whom I have quoted in this chapter several times. His excellent book, *Web Pages That Suck* (Sybex, Inc., 1998), coauthored with Mike Wills, and its equally excellent sequel, *Son of Web Pages That Suck* (Sybex, Inc., 2002), which he wrote solo, provide guidance that Web designers ignore at their peril.[13] You can nominate really bad Web sites for his "Daily Sucker" Web column in which he lambastes a new site each day by publicly pointing out exactly what's wrong with it and why. I wonder what it must feel like to be the Web master of a site that wins that award. Flanders doesn't e-mail the offending sites, but writes that "…we have some psychos who enjoy e-mailing the offending sites and informing them their site made WPTS." Well, count me as a psycho (but you knew that already, didn't you?). When I nominate a site, I do it because that site annoyed me, and when it wins I want to rub the offender's nose in it, deliberately and with malice afore-thought. And I try to send it to the president of the company, some-times going so far as to print a hard copy and send it to him by UPS overnight delivery (as long as I'm not in Sweden). "Congratulations!" I say in my e-mail. "Your Web site really sucks. In fact, on the entire Web, Vincent Flanders couldn't find a suckier one to show off today. So you're immortalized on WebPagesThatSuck.com! Have a nice day." It tends to wake them up to smell the coffee. Or it would, if only they could find the nearest Starbucks. But alas, it's six miles away, so Starbucks.com won't tell them where it is. Too bad Kinko's doesn't sell coffee. I wonder if they'd do it in Swedish.

---

13. Chapter 2

3

. . .

KEEP ME SAFE

Slammer worm! Code Red virus! Batten down the hatches! Shut down on the date that the Michelangelo virus is scheduled to explode. Spyware logging your keystrokes and stealing your passwords and credit card numbers. Modem hijackers dialing 900 numbers that you get charged for. It seems that not a day goes by that we don't hear of another Very Bad Thing happening on our computer.

When I was a boy listening to "Peter and the Wolf," I scared the snot out of my little brother by telling him that the wolf was going to come out of the record and eat him up. I'd probably prefer the lupine creature to the bad guys that can crawl through the Internet pipe into my daughter's very bedroom. Afraid? You should be. Very.

This chapter does not give specific instructions for how to secure your computer or network. Any number of good articles will tell you about firewalls and virus scanners and the like.[1] Instead, I'll take you into the process of thinking about security and designing it into programs. I'll show you the sorts of problems that software developers need to solve and the ways in which they accomplish it,

---

1. Some of the best are from the Computer Emergency Response Team at Carnegie-Mellon University, online at www.cert.org.

or fail to. I hope to get you to the point where you can understand for yourself what makes sense in security terms, and what's a bunch of nonsense spewed out by irresponsible vendors to obscure the fact that they don't know what they're talking about and are foisting dangerous programs on you.

THE WAY IT WAS

The world has always contained, and probably always will contain, bad guys that want to harm you. Sometimes the reasons are economic—junkies want to steal your car stereo for their next fix, and organized-crime chop shops want to steal your whole car. Sometimes they're ideological—an eco-zealot wants to disable your Hummer so that it won't run over any more spotted owls, or a terrorist wants to bring the Great Satan to its knees. And sometimes the bad guys want to smash your windshield just to show that they can. You can't completely eliminate these risks, but you reduce them to levels that you're willing to tolerate, usually by staying away from the kinds of places where these people hang out. When you do have to go there, you pay money to park your car in a supervised place, or do your best to find someplace at least well lit and open to public view. And if that's not possible, you take a taxi, or limit the loss by driving there in your clunker car that not even the Salvation Army will accept as a donation.

In the early days of desktop computing, the bad guys couldn't easily get onto your computer. Which was good, because early versions of DOS and Windows and the applications that ran on them contained no security at all. Software developers were comfortable, or more accurately their customers were comfortable, that as long as they kept their PCs physically locked up, bad guys couldn't sneak onto the PCs and do bad things. The computer behaved more or less like any other expensive electronic box, such as your large-screen TV, and you secured it in similar, familiar ways. Your greatest worry was having to spend money to replace it if it ever got stolen.

That approach worked because we used our computers mostly for running stand-alone applications, like the text-based dungeon adventure game Zork. We didn't often connect to other computers. And when we did, it was in direct ways that were relatively secure. For example, when I used automatic bill payment with CheckFree back in 1990, my computer used a telephone modem to dial CheckFree's number directly. No bad guy could eavesdrop on a transaction without tapping an analog phone line, which is far more difficult and dangerous than the small amount of money stolen would warrant.

Even as networking spread to the corporate environment and computers in workplaces got tied intimately together, security wasn't an enormous problem because most programs and data came from trustworthy sources. The information systems staff installed new programs, so you didn't have to worry whether they contained spy programs (other than the ones that allowed your boss to keep track of you goofing off, and there's not much you can do about that). The data documents and e-mail that you worked on came from internal colleagues, so you were pretty sure they didn't contain software bombs (other than inadvertent bugs caused by bad programmers, and there's not much you can do about that either, then or now). Companies had to block access to some sensitive data, such as employee salary tables, but this was a much smaller problem than it is today, and was often solved by putting the sensitive data on its own separate computing environment that wasn't connected to the rest of the company. (My editor won't let me include the exact words of the company comptroller when I asked him for a login account on his stand-alone payroll system.)

WHY IT SUCKS TODAY

The Internet changed everything. It connected every intelligent box in the world to every other intelligent box in the world. It enormously lowered the friction of communicating between good guys—say, you and Amazon.com—so it shouldn't be any surprise that it did the same for bad guys as well.

The bad guys in cyberspace want to harm your computer for the same reasons that they want to harm your car: to make money, to influence societal behavior, or just because. They do this through running their programs on your computer, or stealing your sensitive data, or some combination of the two. There are three main ways in which the Internet makes this type of crime easier to commit and harder to guard against than it is in the physical world.

The first is that the Internet has done away with distance as an impediment to crime. A bad guy from, say, Romania can't easily break into your car in New York City, but the Internet will mindlessly carry his attack data to your computer if he points it there, or if you inadvertently request it, thinking it's something interesting and benign. If it's the right data and you haven't locked the door, he can break in from 5,000 miles away as easily as from next door. Frances Cairncross wrote a book called *The Death of Distance* (Harvard Business School Press, 2001), in which she discussed the consequences of the Internet's cheap, fast data communication, but I don't recall that this was one of them.

The second is that Internet attacks consume much less of the attacker's time than they do in the physical universe. It takes minutes to smash the window on a car and jimmy out the stereo, then hours to go and sell it for a fix. It takes a second or less to try to crack into a computer. The Internet bad guy can attack many more targets than the physical car thief in the same amount of time, increasing the probability that he'll find one that's vulnerable.

The third is that the Internet allows attack tools to spread much more quickly than they do in the physical world. It's very difficult for, say, a safecracker to communicate to other thieves his feel for the tumblers in a lock. But on the Internet, only one very smart bad guy needs to figure out the original crack. He can then make software tools for exploiting that break, and distribute them almost instantly to almost anyone. This allows many more bad guys, nowhere near as skilled as the original one, to take advantage of it. Attacks can spread much more rapidly, as infectious diseases spread more rapidly in these days of jet aircraft than they could in the days of sailing ships.

These force multipliers add up. A major financial company once told me that its main Web site regularly receives more than a hundred attacks *per second*. This sounds like an enormous amount, at least it did to me. Nevertheless, the Internet is economically compelling. Yes, the financial company has to fight off those 100 attacks every second while still providing decent response time to its customers. But it costs that company about $25 when a customer moves money from one account to another by calling a human representative, and a only few cents when they do it online. When you do a million of them a day, the savings more than pay for some of the world's top computer security guys (whom that company does indeed have).

Our computers need to live in a nasty, nasty world. Our security needs are high, and too often programs fail to meet them. We'll never get absolute security; the trade-offs and costs would be too high, as I describe later in this chapter. But through careful thought and good design, we can get it down to a level we can live with. Conceptually, what you need to do is put a condom on your network connections (see Figure 3–1).

The security problems in the modern computing industry come from two main sources. The first, as usual, is that most programmers don't know what they're doing when it comes to security. It's a highly specialized field, and they're generalists. Almost no one currently in the industry has studied it in college, because it hasn't been taught there. It's just now starting to appear in a few computer science curricula, mostly (not always, Bob) taught by instructors without much experience in the field. Almost everyone in upper management in the software industry today reached that level in the days when whiz-bang features, such as a paper clip's dancing eyebrows, were the key to promotion. They find security boring and

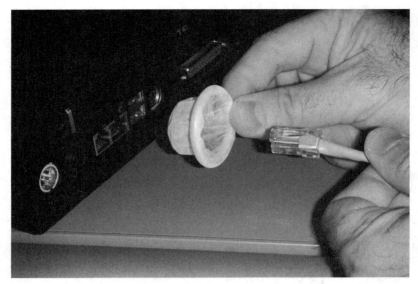

FIGURE 3-1 Here's what you really need to do with your computer.

distracting. They wish those scruffy security guys down the hall, weird even by geek standards, would just make it go away so that they could go back to doing the fun stuff.

Defensive thinking runs contrary to the usual programmer mindset, and they don't like it. You can see that in their own description of what they do: "attack problems." They take a problem apart, figure it out, then concentrate their efforts on the point of attack until they crack it. The defensive mindset is a very different thing, difficult to get into and difficult to maintain. *Defensive thinking* has even become a derogatory term: "You've got a Maginot mentality, you hopeless wimp."[2] Try watching a live hockey game sometime, keeping your eye

2. The Maginot Line was a series of heavy fortifications built by France after World War I along her border with Germany to repel any future invasions. Instead of suicidally charging straight into its teeth when they attacked in 1940, the unobliging Germans merely rolled around the northern end of it through unfortified Belgium and took the rest of France, then waited for the troops inside the Maginot Line to get hungry and surrender.

only on your team's defensemen. First, you'll notice that it's almost impossible for you to do this for more than a few seconds. Your brain keeps dragging your eyes toward the moving puck and the action around it. When you force yourself, you'll see that the defensemen play a completely different game than the attacking forwards. They wait, they watch, they think ahead, they position themselves in advance of where they think the action will move. And in the second period, try watching only the goaltender, the ultimate defensive player. Unless you're his mother or a goaltender yourself (or both), you can't do it. At all. So it shouldn't surprise anyone that the people who've trained and practiced all of their lives as slashing attack forwards find it very difficult to change into something else.

The second, more serious, problem is that even the programmers who do understand the technology of security think in terms of that technology and not in terms of the people using it. They consider the user to be an annoying distraction from their cool equations, as too many hyperscientific doctors think of the patient as an unpleasant side effect of an interesting disease. The programmers think that if they just get their internal strategies right, everything will work out perfectly. *Wrong!* Security, as with just about everything in computing, is more of a people problem than it is a technical problem, as I'll show you later in this chapter. Security guru Bruce Schneier says that security is a process, not a product. It is a chain, and like any chain, is only as strong as the weakest link. And I'll add that until the design process recognizes and understands and accounts for the fundamental humanity of the user, this is where the weakest link will always be and this is where the chain will always break. Come; let me show you some examples.

WHAT PROGRAMMERS NEED TO KNOW, BUT DON'T

As I've said many times, security is a highly specialized field of which the average application programmer is ignorant. Worse, he doesn't recognize that ignorance or its consequences. He says to himself, "Hey, I'll figure out that security stuff when I get there, same as I do for everything else." That doesn't work anymore; the bad guys are too smart and too dedicated to their black art. ("They don't have girlfriends," laments one application programmer I know. "They don't eat, they don't sleep. All they do is hack. How can we win against them?") Here's an example of doing it wrong because the programmer didn't know any better. It's from a project I worked on in my formative days, going on 20 years ago. Hear my confession:

I worked at the time for a company, now defunct and unlamented, that built foreign exchange trading systems for major banks. We didn't sell too many, hence the "defunct" bit, but a few of them went to banks with names you would recognize even today, after 20 years of mergers. The traders would start their workdays, as do all knowledge workers in the world, by logging into their terminals with a user ID and password. These would be sent over the network to the central server to prove the trader's identity, after which the server would allow him to enter deals.

Here's the catch. A device exists called a **packet sniffer,** which allows anyone to read and record all the data that passes by on the network to which it's attached. Packet sniffers are easy to come by. Many are simply programs that run on a regular PC, reconfiguring and using its network connection in ways that most programs don't. They have many legitimate uses, including security audits and program development, so banning them isn't possible. Besides, as I'm sure my National Rifle Association member readers will leap to point out, when packet sniffers are outlawed, only outlaws will sniff packets.

The network ran only inside the bank and wasn't connected to anything outside, so we didn't have to worry about some bad guy two continents away listening in. Even so, any banker will tell you that inside theft jobs are the most dangerous, and that banks place all kinds of safeguards and audits into their procedures to prevent and detect them.[3] A computer plugged anywhere in hundreds of yards of cable could have read the foreign exchange network traffic. It would be impossible to find a bad guy's connection in all that wire, passing as it does through walls and ceilings, especially when the packet sniffer program could be running on a computer that's authorized to be on the network but not to run that program.

Suppose we send the password over the network in clear text, as shown in Figure 3–2. A bad guy with a packet sniffer could read the password, steal it, then log on and enter deals as though he were the authorized trader. Clearly this can't be allowed. My boss at the time was a good application programmer and generally quite smart, but he didn't know about security. He came up with the strategy shown in Figure 3–3. He figured that he'd scramble the password before sending it (a), using a mathematical operation known as a **hash.** A hash operation is a mathematical mixing-up function that is easy to calculate forward but impossible to work backward, in a manner similar to mixing paint or scrambling an egg. The client would send the hashed password over the network instead of in clear text. A bad guy who read the packet containing the hash wouldn't be able to work backward to the clear text because of the one-way nature of the hash function. Meanwhile, the server would calculate the hash value using the password it expected from that user (b). If it matched the one that the user sent, then the user must have started with the correct password and therefore must really be the trader he's claiming to be. If not, then he isn't.

Unfortunately, that didn't solve the problem, because the value of the hashed password would never change as long as the clear-text

---

3. For example, I once wandered into a bank's trading room to look at a computer that was having trouble and found the traders discussing sensitive strategy. I was required to remain in the room until they had finished their discussion and announced the results into the market, lest I use what I'd overheard to their detriment. "We don't distrust you more than anyone else, Plattski," they said, "but business is business. And if it does get spilled, trust us; you do *not* want to be a suspect. Just sit over there away from the phone, read the newspaper, and keep your hands where we can see them until we're finished." I did.

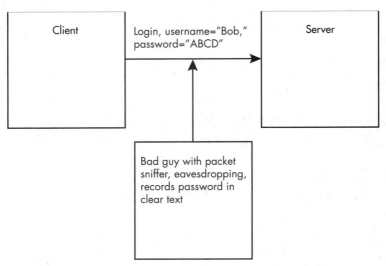

FIGURE 3-2 Sending a password in clear text; not a good idea

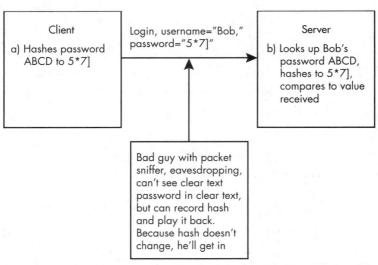

FIGURE 3-3 Sending a password hashed; looks plausible, but is vulnerable to a recording attack

password didn't. All a bad guy had to do was to record the hashed password and write a program that played that same value back to the server, a trivial operation. I actually did a recording/playback attack of exactly this type, after the company went belly up, for a customer bank that wanted to add some features to the now-orphaned product. I had never worked on that part of the software before, and I'm not the smartest guy in the world, but it took me only about 20 minutes, ten of which I spent figuring out where to plug in the packet sniffer. When I saw the first login packets going by, I said to myself, "It can't be *that* simple, can it?" Ah, but it could be, and it was. The trading system had no security whatsoever in the face of a not-all-that-determined attack by a not-all-that-bright attacker with physical access to the network wire, because its designer didn't have the necessary skills to do it properly.

A secure way of sending passwords isn't hard to design once you understand the problem, as you now do, dear reader. The hash value needs to vary randomly from one login to the next, as shown in Figure 3–4. The client sends a login request to the server (a), containing his username but not his password. The server responds with a large random number, called the **challenge** (b), that's different every time. The client combines the challenge number with his password. He then performs the hash operation on the combination and sends the result (c), as in the previous example. Meanwhile, the server performs the same combination and calculates the result, again as before (d). If they match, then the client must have started with correct password *and* challenge number, and therefore must really be who he says he is.

Eavesdropping on this login session won't help the bad guy very much. He can't just play it back as he did in the first example, because at the next login request, the challenge number will be different, and hence so will the hash containing the correct password. The only way to attack this system is with brute force. The bad guy would go to a separate computer and step through every possible clear-text password, combining it with the original challenge number and running the result through the hash function, until the result matched the hash result that he recorded. (He wouldn't try this on the production system because almost any login system,

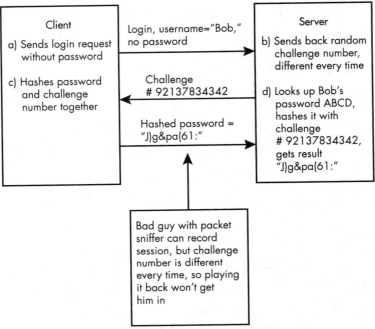

FIGURE 3-4 Handshaking used for authentication. The challenge number is different every time, so the hash value is different every time. This is not vulnerable to a recording attack (which doesn't mean that it's safe).

even one this weak, knows enough to lock out a user's account after a few failed logins to thwart that type of attack.) He'd then know that he had found the user's clear-text password, and he'd go back to the bank's network to log in with it. But if the password is long enough and random enough, it would take the attacker thousands of years to check all the alternatives, by which time we probably wouldn't care very much.

This type of login operation, known as **handshaking,** isn't difficult to program once you realize that's what you have to do, nor does it take much time to run when you're logging in. My boss didn't understand it, and he didn't understand that he didn't understand it. He shouldn't have been designing security systems, and neither should anyone else at that company, including me.

Fortunately, to the best of my knowledge, no bank has used this system in more than a decade (hence the "unlamented" bit). I hope I'm right.

Every time you read of a new security hole being discovered in some program, it's because a programmer made a mistake of this sort and another programmer found it. The errors are usually subtler than the one I've shown here, and often in parts of the program other than the login. But it's this kind of thing, for this kind of reason.

A HUMAN OPERATION

Now you understand at least a little of secure program design, more than a guy who was doing it for a living not that long ago did. (Scary thought, ain't it?) But security encompasses much more than just technology. Bruce Schneier wrote a book on **cryptography** (the making and cracking of codes and ciphers) titled *Applied Cryptography* (Wiley, 1995), which is highly regarded in its field. Seven years later, he recanted, in a book titled *Secrets and Lies: Digital Security in a Networked World*, which begins: "I wrote this book to correct a mistake. [*Applied Cryptography*] described a mathematical utopia. I talked about cryptography as if it were The Answer™.

"The result wasn't pretty. Readers believed that cryptography was a kind of magic security dust that they could sprinkle over their software and make it secure.... A colleague once told me that the world was full of bad security systems designed by people who had read *Applied Cryptography*." When he started designing and analyzing security systems for customers, he "found that the weak points had nothing to do with the mathematics. They were in the hardware and the software, the networks, and the people. Beautiful pieces of mathematics were made irrelevant through bad programming, a lousy operating system, or someone's bad password choice." He sums up by saying, "If you think technology can solve your security problems, then you don't understand the problems and you don't understand the technology." I couldn't agree more.

I showed you in the previous example how programmers could make mistakes that would lead to the easy compromise of their systems. Now I'll show you how, even if the programmer gets what he considers to be his part of it right, a user can still break the system by doing just what human beings normally do.

At the end of the last section, I said that the bad guy would have to crack the hashed password with a brute force attack, running every conceivable password through the hash function. It wouldn't take him too long to figure out which hash function the system used; there aren't many with the proper mathematical properties and their fingerprints are distinctive to an expert. That's not where security comes from. Instead, security comes from the number of possible passwords the bad guy would have to try. If the password had six letters, as ours did, he'd have to check everything from AAAAAA to ZZZZZZ, more than 300 million different combinations. Let the password contain numbers as well as letters and you're up to 2 billion possibilities. Use eight characters rather than six and you have almost 3 trillion. Let lowercase letters be different from uppercase, add punctuation characters, and you have a quadrillion or so different possibilities. Trying them all would take the bad guy more than 31,000 years if he could check 1,000 per second. Change the password once or twice a year and you don't have to worry much about a brute force attack.

But if the bad guy is smart, he'll think about the human factor at work in the choice of password. Not all passwords are equally likely. Passwords are generally chosen by human users, whose minds work in terms of linguistic words. A human is unable to pull a random password out of his brain no matter how hard he tries. So the smart bad guy will use what's called a **dictionary attack** rather than brute force. He won't just try AAAAAA, then AAAAAB, then AAAAAC, and so on. He'll figure that since a user chose the password, it's probably an actual word, and therefore exists in a dictionary somewhere. He'll find a list of common words (there are many on the Web) and try them one after another: AARON, ABACUS, ACTIVE, and so on. The average human has a working vocabulary of 5,000 words or so, not counting my own coinages of idoit (Chapter 1) and marketingbozo (Chapter 6). At 1,000 combinations per second, same as the first example—I'll let you do the math. A bad password choice reduces the cracking time from 31,000 years to five seconds.[4] Even using two words stacked together, like the first password CompuServe assigned me ("elvesoffend"), the bad guy will still crack it in less than seven hours.

What we really need here is for the passwords to be completely random, like k!&wLa or b8I2=o. These are not hard to generate; any number of utility programs or Web sites can do that for you. Because the foreign exchange system was used in a bank, with billions of dollars changing hands every day, it probably should have been designed to assign the user a randomly generated password. It would allow him to reset it to another randomly generated password at any time, but wouldn't allow him to change it to a specific one that he wanted.

That approach has drawbacks, obviously. It's very hard for a human to remember a random password, particularly when it's not used very often or he has more than one of them. Since using this application is the trader's main job and he logs in at least twice per day (start of day and after lunch), he'd be able to remember it if he wanted to badly enough and we didn't change it very often, perhaps twice a year. We'd have to fight the trader's natural tendency to write the password down on paper by threatening him with the loss of his coveted and highly paid job if he did so. We'd then have to make examples by periodically searching traders' desks for written

---

4. Some users think they'll protect their passwords by making them foreign language words. At five seconds per 5,000-word vocabulary, the bad guy can check all of the 404 languages on the International Standards Organization list, from Abkhazian to Zuni, in about half an hour. In practice, he'd check the most common dozen or so. In the unlikely event that none of them worked, he'd try cracking the next trader.

passwords and firing the ones we caught with them. Since traders already understand and comply with many other safeguards on confidential information, they'd probably swallow this one as well.

Such a high level of password security would be much more difficult to obtain, and much less appropriate, for most consumer Web sites—say, an online magazine subscription or even a retail shopping site. A retail customer will not tolerate anywhere near the amount of hassle that a highly paid employee will, and the cost of a security breach is much less. Ordinary users can't remember very many random passwords, arguably none. If you try to force them, they'll write the password down on a Post-it Note and stick it to their monitors, or go to a different merchant whose site is easier to use. Fortunately, an individual merchant account is much less attractive to a bad guy than a major bank's foreign exchange operations, and the consequences of a security failure much less costly.

BUDGETING FOR HASSLES

The only completely safe computer is one that's disconnected from any network, turned off, sealed in concrete, and buried ten feet in the ground. Since these tend not to be very useful for getting work done, any sort of actual computer usage involves some level of compromise between utility and security. Choosing the right level of trade-off for an application is the difference between success and failure of a project. If the rules are too lenient, then they don't protect strongly enough and any inconvenience that you cause is wasted. If the rules are too strict, then users either dump the product or come up with some way to bypass them.

I've coined the term *hassle budget* to describe this problem. The hassle budget is the amount of security-related overhead that a user will tolerate in order to use a product. It will vary greatly from one type of product to another and one type of user to another. Program designers should use as much of it as they need to get the job done, but no more.

You can see a clear example in the clock on the lower right-hand corner of the Windows task bar. If you double-click on it, you might see the clock-calendar screen shown in Figure 3–5, showing you, and allowing you to set, the system's current time and date.

I find this very handy when I'm on the phone with prospective clients discussing the dates of future business meetings. I need to quickly know which day of the week is November 23 or which date is a week from Monday, and this box tells me graphically and immediately. The problem is, however, that only users who are designated as administrators on their systems are allowed to see this box. My wife, for example, is not an administrator on our home system (may the gods protect us from that). So if I need to check a future date while I'm sitting at her computer, and I double-click on the clock to bring up this box, I get an annoyance message (I won't call it an error message; I didn't make any error, the stupid programmer who wrote this did) saying, "You do not have the proper privilege level to change the system time."(See Figure 3–6.) So to bring up the calendar, I have to go back to the start menu, pick Start, Programs, Accessories, Idoicy, Hassle, Numbskulls ... (you get the idea).

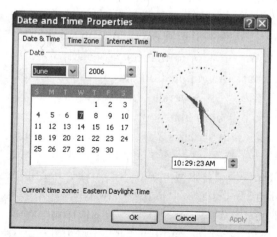

FIGURE 3-5 Clock-calendar from double-clicking on the digital clock in the lower right-hand corner of Windows XP

FIGURE 3-6 Message box disallowing the user to change the clock

Allowing only administrators to change the system clock is probably reasonable. The proper operation of many programs depends on the computer's internal date and time being correct, and restricting the ability of changing it to people who know what they're doing is not a bad idea. But blocking a nonadministrator user from even seeing the calendar and clock is dumb. The data isn't that sensitive; I mean we're not trying to prevent users from knowing what date it will be next Thursday. A nonadministrator user should be allowed to see the box, but somehow be informed that it's read-only—maybe gray out the OK button, maybe an explanatory string, maybe an entirely different dialog box designed for display only. This designer has not spent the user's hassle budget wisely.

Once a user feels that her hassle budget has been exceeded, she'll find a way to bypass whatever rules the programmer has established, probably without distinguishing the wise ones from the stupid ones. She doesn't know how to do that, or especially want to know how, and anyway, that's the application designer's job. In this clock-calendar example, users will designate themselves as administrators so that they can see this box. That sounds reasonable from a user's perspective, but it actually violates a security principle called the Principle of Least Privilege. This states that a user should always have the lowest level of privilege that will allow her to get her work done so that if she does get hacked by a bad guy, the damage is less than it otherwise would be. If a bad guy takes over a system whose user has administrative privileges, he can trash any file on the disk, whereas if he takes over a system whose user has a lower level of privilege, he can probably only trash the logged-in user's files. This is especially important in family situations where many users share the same computer. A casual user can't be expected to know this principle and shouldn't be tempted by convenience to violate it.

The programmer who wrote this particular piece of code would no doubt say, "The user shouldn't be doing that, casual calendar viewing isn't what that dialog box is for." That's precisely the attitude that needs to change. It's the programmer's job to adjust to the user, not the other way around. The user found that functionality useful and convenient. It's the programmer's job to make it safe.

Here's another, bloodier example: Many years ago I worked for a company that made chaff radar decoys for ships and aircraft. We started with meter-long bundles of aluminized fiberglass strands, then chopped them to the half-wavelength of the radar we wanted to block (usually a few centimeters) using a power-fed press with a guillotine blade. This device had two safety interlock switches located far enough apart that the operator couldn't hold them both with the same hand at the same time, and it wouldn't run unless both buttons were pressed simultaneously. The machine's designer thought that this layout would keep the operator's hands clear of the blade while it was chopping. However, one particular user liked to smoke while operating the machine. (This was back in the days when people were allowed to smoke in factories.) She made herself a stick with two tabs on it the proper distance apart. She'd lay it down with one tab on each button, apply pressure with one hand, and smoke with the other. She got quite good at extracting, lighting, and puffing a coffin nail single-handedly. She felt that her hassle budget had been exceeded, so she figured out a workaround. I hope she can find a prosthetic hand with a cigarette holder attachment.

USERS ARE LAZY

If there's one quality that defines human beings, particularly of the computer-using variety, it's laziness. In fact, I would argue that laziness is the third-highest determinant of human behavior, right behind hunger and horniness.[5] As I wrote in Chapter 1, most programmers drive stick-shift cars, and almost none of their users do. Users only want to get a specific task done: read the news so that they don't have to buy a paper, order groceries so that they don't have to go out shopping, play and steal music and videos to avoid buying them, download dirty pictures because they don't have a date for the weekend. They haven't the slightest interest in the computer for its own sake, as they don't have the slightest interest in the car for its own sake. They'd be much happier if they could snap their fingers and get their stuff done without either of them. As they don't change the oil on their cars or check the tire pressure like they're supposed to, and wouldn't have them inspected if it wasn't state law, so they won't do anything to keep their computers secure unless they're forced to. Good program design takes that into account, and automatically secures everything that it can. Understanding and harnessing the laziness of users worked for book clubs, so it ought to work for software developers as well. Here's an example of doing it wrong, then fixing it.

In the early years, software companies released new versions of their applications more or less annually. Each release contained new features and fixes to bugs caused by the previous year's features (and fixes to bugs caused by fixes to the previous year's bugs, etc.). Once we started going online and getting attacked through the Internet, that time schedule was nowhere near fast enough. Once a security hole is discovered, hopefully by a good guy, the manufacturer has to fix it right away before bad guys start using it for attacks. This is generally done by means of a **patch,** a small piece of software that you download from the application vendor's Web site and install on your

---

5. I had originally placed laziness in second place, behind hunger. Then a friend who was reviewing this manuscript asked me, "Would you mow the lawn this afternoon if it meant getting sex tonight?" The next time a self-righteous mathematics snob says that you can't compare apples to oranges, try that one on him.

computer. It's usually not a whole new version of the program, but just a small replacement piece with the vulnerability fixed.

The problem is that patches, like seat belts and birth control, work only if you use them, and almost nobody does of his own accord. Vendors would post patches on a Web site, occasionally announcing their availability to registered users via e-mail. Apart from the large percentage of users who had either changed e-mail addresses or never registered at all, almost no one receiving the e-mail took the trouble to go to the site, find the correct patches among all the other garbage (I find Hewlett-Packard's to be especially difficult to navigate, although in fairness they have many, many products to support), download them, and install them, running the risk of the patch breaking something else.

The consequences of relying on users to keep their patches current can be severe. For example, the Slammer worm that hit database servers on January 25, 2003, crashing many of them and almost bringing down the whole Internet, wouldn't have happened with proper patch management. Microsoft had released a patch for it three months previously; a good patch that fixed the problem and didn't break anything else. The computers that got hit didn't have that patch installed, including several at Microsoft, even though the program that got hit generally requires a professional administrator whose job is to keep up-to-date on such things. If even Microsoft-employed professionals won't keep up-to-date on its patches, what chance do the rest of us have? None. Zero. Nada.

Microsoft then did what antivirus vendors have done for years, which is provide automatic updates. The Windows Update Service first became available as an add-on update itself, which meant that almost no one made the effort to find it, install it, and use it. However, it's now built into Windows XP Service Pack 2, and you have to go out of your way to turn it off. Every now and then it checks Microsoft's site for updates, and downloads and installs the ones that it finds. The next version of Microsoft's tools for developers will allow application programmers to do the same thing cheaply and easily for the products they build. The main problem will be that, if an automatically installed patch breaks a program's existing functionality, the company will be flooded with expensive tech-support phone calls. That prospect ought to ensure that they test updates thoroughly.

The laziness of users also becomes important when deciding which pieces of Windows to enable by default, and which to require explicit user action to enable. If you depend on users to take active steps to secure their machines, they won't. For example, it used to be common for software to ship with a built-in administrator account with a password of "admin," which the administrator was supposed to change. An astonishing number of them never did so. Hey, I didn't, until I got hacked by a Web virus that guessed that password. Richard Feynman, the Nobel physicist, described laziness in his autobiography as the third major way in which he cracked safes for fun. (Finding it written down around the user's desk was first, and guessing important dates in the owner's life was second.) Most safes are shipped with a default combination, like $0 - 25 - 0$ or $25 - 50 - 25$. Customers are supposed to change it, but many didn't. It's much more secure to ship software with most of its functionality disabled, and allow users to turn on only what they need, than it is to have everything turned on and rely on users to disable what they don't need. Again, the drawback is that users will call a vendor's tech-support line when the functionality that they know the program has doesn't work at the first try. Answering the phone to tell them, "Yeah, you have to click here and choose a password to explicitly turn that on," is expensive. It's not enough from a technical standpoint to disable functionality by default. Vendors have to think carefully about how to help users turn on the pieces that they need to, safely and easily.

My work with hassle budgets and lazy users (a redundancy, the opposite of an oxymoron, there isn't any other kind of user) has led me to coin Platt's Third Law of the Universe, which states simply that "Laziness Trumps Everything." If something is easy to do, people will do it frequently whether they should or not, and if it's hard to do, then they'll do it infrequently, whether they should or not. Therefore, a smart program designer will make good, smart, safe things easy to do; and bad, dumb, dangerous things hard to do. The designer of the clock/calendar dialog box would do well to take this into account.

SOCIAL ENGINEERING

My college physics professor once posed a challenge to my class: dream up as many ways as we could of measuring the height of a building using a barometer. Apart from the obvious one of measuring the difference in air pressure between the top and the bottom, our chemically enhanced brainstorming session produced many others: throw the barometer off the top and measure the time it takes to fall, measure the difference in its weight as it moves farther from the Earth's center of mass, and so on. But the easiest and most accurate way we thought of was to go to the owner and say, "Hey, I'll give you this perfectly good barometer if you tell me how tall your building is."

That's often the easiest way to crack a system—just ask the user nicely. It's also the hardest for software vendors to defend against, because it bypasses anything they have control over. The art of cracking security by asking nicely is called **social engineering**. You'd be surprised how often it works.

The arch hacker Kevin Mitnick, convicted and sent to jail for cracking systems, testified before Congress in 2000. His testimony said, "I was so successful in [social engineering] that I rarely had to resort to a technical attack.... Companies can spend millions of dollars toward technological protections and that's wasted if somebody can basically call someone on the telephone and either convince them to do something on the computer that lowers the computer's defenses or reveals the information they were seeking." His book, *The Art of Deception: Controlling the Human Element of Security* (Wiley, 2002), details a number of his favorite techniques.

For example, suppose a social engineer has acquired your company phone directory and an organization chart, perhaps by sorting through your trash (**dumpster diving,** it's called). You might receive a phone call with a female voice (people always trust women more than men) saying, "Hi, Bob, this is Sarah [correct name for the admin person, found on the org chart]. I work for Mr. Franklin [your boss's boss's boss, again, correct name from the chart]. I think we met at the Christmas party last year. [You didn't, but who can remember, and who'd be so rude as to say so, especially to such a delicious voice?] We're over at that new prospect's office [an earlier call to the big cheese confirms he's out of town] and we need your help. I can't log in to the company system from here and we really need the [big important project] file. Can you e-mail it to—[voice off] Mr. Franklin, what's that address again? [back to the phone]— thisguy@seemsplausible.com. Thanks so much, you've been a big help. I'll make sure to tell Mr. Franklin. 'Bye."

Who could resist that? The caller obviously knows your company and its operations. She clearly must be legitimate. Think of the chance to ingratiate yourself with higher-ups, and the consequences if you refuse. That's social engineering. You might think that this has nothing to do with computer security. But the great pains that you take to protect your information are rendered useless by a little sweet talk. We've found the weakest link of the chain, and until you secure it, all your great technology is useless.

Shocked? You shouldn't be. Never misunderestimate the power of human stupidity. A similar technique would probably work for stealing user IDs and passwords. "I know not to do that, Plattski!" you shout. "You think I'm dumb or something?" But presenting your user ID and password to someone isn't unusual. You do that every time you log in. All the bad guy has to do is to set up a situation in which you think you're dealing with a legitimate request for your credentials, even though you aren't.

Figure 3–7 shows an example that many people got in an e-mail a few years ago. It purports to come from PayPal.com, the online

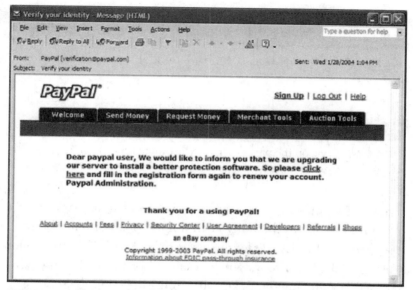

FIGURE 3-7 Phishing attack

money transfer service, but it's really from a bad guy. The "From:" e-mail address says PayPal.com, as you can see. Most users don't realize that this address doesn't specify where the message really came from. You can put in anything as the "From:" address on an e-mail, just as you can write any return address on a snail-mail letter you send. Usually you put the correct thing there to help return messages that go astray, but not in this case. The actual sending history, the postmark if you will, is buried in the e-mail headers that this program isn't showing. The format of the message matches PayPal's online look and feel because the bad guy has simply copied it from the PayPal.com Web site. All the links except the one that says "click here" point to actual PayPal.com pages. If you click on that link, it takes you to a site with an address that looks like PayPal (it was ebay-paypal.com, if memory serves) but, again, really belongs to the bad guy. The only easily discernible difference is that the little lock in the lower right-hand corner, distinguishing a secure site, is on the page itself (see Figure 3–8) instead of on the browser's status

FIGURE 3-8 Lock on browser status bar indicating a secure connection to the server

FIGURE 3-9 Lock on the page itself, not the browser status bar, untruthfully claiming a secure connection

bar (see Figure 3–9). This may seem like an obvious error, but it's difficult to notice in the noisy environment of a normal Web page (see Figure 3–10). Except for the errors in language ("Thank you for a using PayPal!"), it looks almost exactly like the real thing. This type of social engineering is known as **phishing** for passwords.

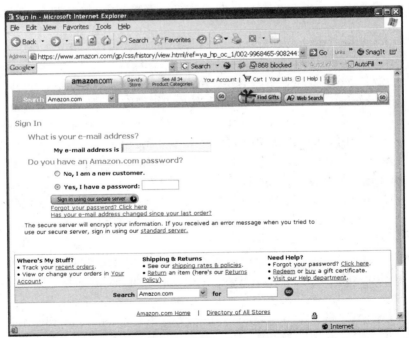

FIGURE 3-10 Lock on the page itself, difficult to recognize in the context of a busy page

This is almost impossible for a software vendor to protect against. Users need to know that they shouldn't trust links in e-mails they receive unsolicited. Even then, instructions telling them to enter the string "ebay-paypal.com" in their browsers would get them to the bad guy's site. Even mighty Citibank (true Web address: citibank.com) is vulnerable to Web addresses that resemble it to a casual eye, such as cittibank.biz, available as of March 1, 2006.

A bad guy probably doesn't even need to masquerade in order to steal passwords. He can spend a hundred bucks buying some content—music videos, porn, whatever—or just steal it. Then he'll set up a Web site with a couple of teasers on the home page, telling users that they need to set up a free account to see the remainder. He'll promise in a (lying) privacy statement that he won't use their information for anything, maybe even adding a verification question to recover a lost password to make the site seem legitimate. He'll then take the user IDs and passwords that users choose and try them on other sites, like Amazon and eBay. Or mutual fund company sites. If the user has reused an ID and password, which is extremely common, the user has given away his security.

Since it's so easy to steal someone's password, you can see why I'm so down on biometric authentication (explained in Chapter 4), even if fingerprint readers get built into the keyboards of ordinary users. Once a bad guy steals a fingerprint you can't ever change it. He doesn't even have to be present to lift your drinking glass or dust your doorknob. All he has to do is ask you to authenticate with the fingerprint reader and send him the file containing the scan. Social engineering is very, very hard to combat with technology. Buy a copy of Mitnick's book if you want to lie awake at night for weeks after you finish reading it. The last book that did that to me was *The Coming Plague: Newly Emerging Diseases in a World Out of Balance,* by Laurie Garrett (Penguin, 1995). Perhaps computer security and hemorrhagic fevers have more to do with each other than I thought.

LAST WORD ON SECURITY

The worst sense of security that you can have is a false one. Let me tell you about a client who will remain nameless, for reasons which will quickly become apparent. The first day I taught at this client, I entered the building among a group of employees, waved my Dunkin' Donuts ten-punch coffee card at the guard as though holding a badge like the others, and walked right through. That's pretty sloppy, even in donut-crazed New England. The next day I decided to sign in at the guard desk just to be nice. The rent-a-cop guard (wearing captain's bars, for heaven's sake) never asked me for ID. She never called the guy I said I was visiting to check whether I was expected. She never noticed that I had signed the register with the name Ted Kaczynski. She just waved me through and said, "Have a nice day, sir." That client would be safer if they took the money they spend on what they call security and burned it on the public common. They'd be no less secure, but at least they wouldn't *think* they're secure when they're not.

I spent the first 15 minutes of that morning's class haranguing the students about their company's complete lack of security and advising them to watch their backs, because the guys who were getting paid to do that for them weren't doing it. And just as I finished my rant, one student said, "Hey, I hope this is a hoax, but I just got this e-mail saying that a plane hit the World Trade Center." "Is it dated April 1?" I asked him, thinking of the now-defunct British humor magazine *Punch*. Legend has it that their headline for April 1, 1919 read: "Archduke Franz Ferdinand Found Alive, War Fought by Mistake."[6] But it was dated September 11. As we all know. That's what a false sense of security leads to ("Boxcutters? No problem. But

---

6. The causes of World War I (1914–1918) were many and complex. But the match that touched off the powder keg was the assassination of Archduke Franz Ferdinand, heir to the Austrian throne, in Sarajevo on June 28, 1914. And while *Punch* was primarily known for its humor, it was the first magazine to publish Dr. John McCrae's distinctly nonhumorous poem, "In Flanders Fields," on December 8, 1915.

nothing dangerous, like a hot Starbucks double latte.") So make sure you don't have one. A false sense of security, that is. You can have a latte if you want; although, like decaf coffee and nonalcoholic beer, I've never quite seen the point.

WHAT YOU CAN DO

Security matters today. It didn't when all we were using was Solitaire and Notepad, but it does now. If you miss those carefree days, well, so do I, but it's part of growing up.

You now know something about computer security. Not enough to design a system, but enough to know when to be worried (frequently), and enough to recognize a snow job when you see one (ditto). If you think you should be worried about something, you probably should.

Mainstream software vendors, not just security product developers, are starting to take notice. In particular, Microsoft seems to be finally getting the message. Bill Gates sent a company-wide e-mail on January 15, 2002, announcing that what he called "Trustworthy Computing" was Microsoft's highest priority. "...Trustworthy Computing is more important than any other part of our work. If we don't do this, people simply won't be willing—or able—to take advantage of all the other great work we do." I've said for years that Microsoft needed to change priorities; that spending one single developer day—nay, one single developer minute—on a paper clip's blinking eyebrows before plugging every possible security hole and fixing every possible crash is to worship false gods.

The press has reported how all the developers in the company underwent security training and then performed a line-by-line code review looking for vulnerabilities. More to the point, my sources inside the company say that there has been a significant change in culture; that security is a part of every design spec written by every developer instead of being slathered on as an afterthought if they get time (and no one anywhere ever *gets* time for anything; you explicitly make time for the stuff that matters most or it doesn't get done); that promotions are being given to managers who make their products more secure rather than fancier. As I've written in other chapters, programmers value peer respect more than any other group I've seen, including doctors and pilots. And that respect, by which I mean a guy whose intelligence you respect looking at what you've done and saying, "Hey, nice job, you're smart," is now starting to go to the guys who catch and fix security bugs rather than the ones that design flashy user interfaces. Still, Microsoft is a large company, with lots of program code that no one now living knows how to maintain. It'll take a while for even the best of efforts to ripple through to the world.

Certainly there are many things that software companies need to do to make you more secure, such as sending out automatic update patches. And you should demand that they do these things, in the same way as you demand better user interfaces. But unlike the user interface awfulnesses that I wrote about in other chapters, security cannot come solely from the software developer. It requires user cooperation as well. For example, Microsoft's current top-of-the-line products, Windows XP Service Pack 2 and Windows Server 2003, are less vulnerable than their earlier Windows 95 and Windows 98 abortions. Any bad guy wanting to cause trouble will target the latter rather than the former, and a user who runs the latter is saying, "I don't care about security. I know there's a much more secure alternative available to me, and I'm choosing not to use it. Do to me as you will."

In his classic book, *How to Win Friends and Influence People* (originally published in 1937), Dale Carnegie lists rule #7 for making your home life happier as "Read a good book on the sexual side of marriage." Security is sort of like that, especially when you consider what the bad guys are trying to do to your computer, and to you. The computing world changes too quickly for books to help you much (except for this one, of course). But you should read one good article every year on security for users, and do the things that it says to do. Upgrade to the strongest operating system. Get a firewall and a virus scanner. Turn on automatic updates, even if they occasionally cause a program to stop working. Because much as I've lambasted software companies for writing sucky software, you need to meet them halfway here.

4

. . .

WHO THE HECK ARE YOU?

Mike, a currency trader at a bank where I once consulted, didn't understand what passwords are for. A loyal alumnus of the University of Wisconsin, Mike always wanted his password to be "Badger," after their annoying mascot. After I reset his password, he'd announce to the trading room, "Hey, guess what, you guys, Plattski just made me a badger again!"

WHERE WE CAME FROM

I can see you grinning at Mike, slapping your forehead like Homer Simpson saying "Doh!" Of course, you know better. Passwords are for authentication, proving to a computer that you really are who you say you are. Typing your user ID and password into your computer is the start of most users' day. It also happens many times throughout your work session as you transact business with various Web sites, even check your e-mail. Passwords are common, seem easy, and ought to be well understood. But their current usage, a separate user ID and password for every computer system you use, doesn't work well in today's computing environment.

WHY IT STILL SUCKS TODAY

A small part of the problem is users who don't get it. This is usually fixable, and more important, usually harms no one except the deserving bonehead himself. In Mike's case, I got the notion through his head by having another trader use Mike's password to mess with his disk in a scary but harmless way. He panicked, I fixed it, he repented and mended his ways. (Not everyone works in an office with that kind of handholding.) But a bigger part comes from developers and software architects who don't understand the requirements and limitations of the security systems they build, or fail to build, into their products. This is much more dangerous because their actions affect everyone who uses their products. Computer security is a highly specialized skill. The average application programmer knows essentially nothing about it, as a primary care physician knows very little about neurosurgery. The main difference is that your internist usually knows better than to start drilling holes in your skull when you come in complaining of a headache, whereas the application programmer more often says, "Cool! Where's the manual?" when assigned a security project that he knows nothing about. Let's just say that I've done it, seen the results, and learned better. Eventually.

Designing security properly requires careful analysis and understanding of user behavior, another thing programmer geeks are famously bad at. I recently sat through a deep technical talk on security, which contained some interesting mathematics. (OK, I'm a geek.) But I put an end to the question-and-answer session when I asked, "Please correct me if I'm wrong, but cool as you think your stuff is, is any of it the slightest bit useful until you stop users from writing their passwords on Post-it Notes stuck to their monitors?" And the speaker had to admit that yes, in that situation your computer would become an expensive paperweight, but that wasn't his problem. I wanted to smack him. The human dimension is the first problem that any security system needs to solve, and very few even attempt it.

Remembering passwords is harder than you think. It wasn't a problem when you had only one computer account, usually at work or school. Today, however, computer accounts and the IDs and passwords they require are breeding like bacteria all over cyberspace. I started counting all the accounts that I have with various Web sites, and came up with the astonishing total of 27. And these are just the ones I could easily find. I probably have at least that many again, stashed away in the dark corners of my disk drive. The next time you sit down at your computer, see how many you have. E-mail. Chat. That music site, and that other music site. Airlines. Orbitz. Your bank and your mutual fund house, each of your credit cards, the phone company. The porn site you hope your spouse doesn't find. I'll bet you have over a dozen. And that means they're impossible to manage in a way that's both secure and usable.

INCOMPATIBLE REQUIREMENTS

Highly paid security gurus pontificate that your password should be random so that a potential thief can't guess it from other material containing information about you—not your spouse's name, or children, or dog, and so on. OK, that makes sense. I've cracked a few by guessing those obvious choices. That's why I always use a random generator when I need to choose a password. Then they'll say that you shouldn't write it down. Again, I can see the logic of this. Finding poorly hidden notes containing lock combinations was one of the ways that Nobel physicist Richard Feynman cracked classified safes while working on the atomic bomb project during World War II. He left goofy notes, which drove the security people bonkers. (See his 1985 autobiography, *Surely You're Joking, Mr. Feynman.*) Then they'll tell you to use a different password for every account you have. Like the other two, it makes sense on its own. If a bad guy gets your password by cracking the lightly defended Boy Scout troop Web site, he won't be able to use that password on your mutual fund

Web site, which is (or had better be) much more strongly guarded. Then finally, they'll tell you to change it periodically so that if someone does steal your password, it won't work for very long.

Each of these ideas makes perfect sense on its own. Unfortunately, human beings cannot physically do all four of these things together. *Our brains aren't built that way; that's why we invented computers.* We can do any two of these things at once, if we're lucky. Telling users to do them all while knowing, *knowing* that they can't, instead of figuring out how to be as secure as you can with what users actually can (and sometimes even will) do, constitutes malpractice. It's like a priest ministering only to people who don't sin—easy but pointless. It avoids having to understand what the problem really is and then grapple with it.

Selecting a password means choosing among incompatible requirements. You can use a random string for a password, not write it down, even change it once in a while, provided that you have to memorize only one (and also provided that you aren't in charge of changing it, because you won't make the effort). Alternatively, you can use as many random strings as you want and change them as often as you want, if you don't mind writing them down somewhere you hope is secure.[1] Or you can use many different ones, not write them down, even change them occasionally, as long as they follow a pattern that your brain can wrap itself around—this quarter they're all fish, next quarter they're all birds, or whatever. The least likely to be hacked is the first choice, one (two or three in exceptionally geeky cases) random, unwritten password for all accounts, although the damage caused by a leak is the greatest of all the choices. That's what most people I know do, and that's probably the safest overall. It's not perfect, but neither are the other choices.

---

1. The *Wall Street Journal* reports that one user tried writing down all of his 30+ passwords on a piece of paper that he would carry in his wallet. However, the list kept growing and soon became unreadable. "I'm thinking that tattoos are the way to go," reported the user. Seems to me that'll work until they need to be changed.

The problem with this approach is that many sites have incompatible requirements for passwords. Some consider the character "A" to be different from the character "a" (this is called **case sensitivity**); others treat them as the same character. Some allow characters besides letters and numbers, such as punctuation, some don't, and still others require at least one of them to make passwords harder for a bad guy to guess. I have one account that not only requires a punctuation character in the password, but also insists that it not be the first or the last character. My faculty login at Harvard Extension requires a six-number password. They won't accept letters (I guess that's one way of deciding the case-sensitivity question), or punctuation, or more or fewer digits than six. If Harvard didn't insist on being different from everyone else, I might just be able to keep their password hidden by changing it to one I've already memorized, but I don't have space in my brain to memorize another one just because they feel like being different. Instead, I keep their letter containing my password tacked up on my office bulletin board in plain sight of anyone who walks in.

For another example, a source reports that at his company, the computer security people recently started requiring users to change their passwords every month, and requiring that each password contain at least one letter and at least one number. It sounds logical, but they obviously haven't thought through the human factors. People can't remember a new random string every month, and employers can't make them. So what do the users at this company actually do? The source reports that they choose a pattern they can remember: the name of the month and year, such as Jan2003, Feb2003, and so on. When a thief guesses or steals one user's password, he'll see a pattern that is probably used by many users, a pattern that he can follow to keep cracking as passwords change. This isn't just a little bit bad, it's really awful, and any computer security guy who thinks this provides *one iota* of security is an idoit. Caveat: Sometimes you will see a security person who does indeed know better doing something stupid to appease a stupid boss who thinks he knows something about security but doesn't. That's arguably why Germany lost World War II. A high-ranking idoit decreed that a scrambler in the Enigma encryption machine could not occupy the same position from one day to the next, because that would be too easy to guess. On the contrary, deducing this rule lowered by two-thirds the number of possible combinations that Alan Turing and his colleagues had to check, to the point where they could just barely accomplish it, sometimes. If not for this rule, much of the Enigma information that British code breakers managed to decrypt would have arrived too late to be tactically useful.

The same problem occurs to a lesser extent with user IDs. When you set up a computer account, you generally have to choose a name, unique among all the others on that system, which will identify you and nobody else. I'm dplatt on one site, but that name was already taken on another site, so I'm daveplatt there, and even that name was taken on a third site, so I have to be daveplatt1 there. I can never remember who I am where. Unlike the password problem, however, a good and easy solution exists if site developers would only use it: An e-mail address makes a fine user ID. It's unique to you, it's easy to remember, and it's the same everywhere. Some industry leaders, such as Amazon.com, do this. But some sites won't allow a user ID to contain the at sign (@) or a period (.), and others won't accept a string that long. There's no excuse for this foolishness on the part of developers. It's actually easier for them to write a program that would accept any characters in the user ID string than to take the time to check for and reject forbidden characters. Some development manager said, "Let's spend our precious time and money to make the user's job harder, and ours no easier, just for the sheer pain of it." That person probably didn't phrase the instructions exactly that way, but that is the result, and her brain is at least one neuron short of a synapse. Storage space can't be the problem, at least not for anyone who thinks. The difference between an eight-character standard user ID and a 64-character e-mail address sounds large, but really isn't in modern computing terms. You can fit more than 60 million of the latter into a dollar's worth of disk space at today's prices, and the cost of disk space is currently falling by about half every year. Enough disk space to hold an e-mail address for each of the 5 billion people on this planet would cost roughly $100 (again, today's cost, and falling rapidly).

Sometimes they'll say it's for security reasons, because many people know what your e-mail address is. This shows they don't understand the problem. A user ID isn't meant to be secure. If it was, then allowing the user ID to show on the screen when the user types it in, instead of obscuring it with asterisks as is usually done for a password, would constitute malpractice. User IDs were used on the earliest systems as the address of e-mail or messenger programs that ran only on that system ("Phone PLATT" is the command you would type.) In fact, they're often displayed on a Web page to indicate to the user that he is in fact logged in (see Figure 4–1). Making Mike's ID Badger rather than his password would have been fine.

A user ID is unique but not secure. A password is secure but not unique. (Although one reader reports that a particular site wouldn't let him use his preferred password because another user already had it. Again, a waste of development dollars for the sole purpose of annoying a user. This actually makes *all* users of this system a little less secure, because it reveals at least one password currently in use.) The combination makes you unique and secure, or at least it should. Nothing gets me angrier than boneheads invoking the mantle of security to cover up their own foolishness. Security is a tax on law-abiding people. Levying this tax unnecessarily, or wasting the results, ought to be a crime.

FIGURE 4-1 The login name of a user is often shown as a personalization feature (see top center).

Bonehead prize: ConsumerReports.com actually did show the user's password in clear text every time she typed it in, for more than a year, even after I told them about it. They've stopped now, but this has been a mortal sin since I've been in the computing business, and probably well before. Even the paper-printing teletypes we used during my freshman year in college would repeatedly overprint the password entry so that a random passerby couldn't see it. Any developer or manager ignorant of this basic fact should not be in charge of security for a major publication, but somehow one was. Fortunately they're not guarding anything valuable of mine. But it makes you wonder who's in charge at each of the many places you do online business with.

Some sites make you use the number of your existing account with them as a login ID because their internal logic is based on it—your frequent flyer number, say, on an airline site. This makes a certain amount of sense when you have an identifier that you use constantly in the context of a long-term and intimate relationship—say, an employee or student ID number on a badge you are required to carry at all times and frequently enter on business-related documents. I don't want anywhere near that close a relationship with an airline or department store. Making the user conform to a programmer's internal implementation, instead of designing an interface that conforms to the user's mental model, is an act of colossal arrogance, albeit one that we see far too much of in this industry. The site programmer is refusing to make your life easier, even though he could. One word to the developers involved: *associate*. Take the user ID and look up the account number. If you're too stupid or lazy to do that, get out of this business before you hurt someone, or someone hurts you. Again, Amazon.com does it well, and there's no excuse for other sites not to live up to that standard.

These examples illustrate what I mean when I say that security is a highly specialized field of which ordinary programmers are mostly ignorant. The only way I, or anyone, can remember all of the separate Web site IDs and passwords that we are forced to have, while keeping them convenient enough to use, is to write them down and keep them near our computer. They're usually stuck to people's monitors, or in extremely high security situations, under the keyboard. I keep all of my travel-related IDs and passwords in one file on my machine; otherwise, I couldn't use travel Web sites. It's as simple as that.

Personal finance programs, such as Quicken and Microsoft Money, also use this technique for storing the IDs and passwords to all the bank and credit accounts that you have to deal with, and they'd be much less useful without this capability. Some password management programs, such as Aha (see Figure 4–2) and RoboForms, exist

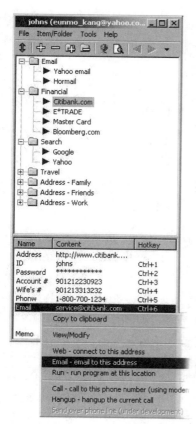

FIGURE 4-2 Aha password storage program

for this purpose. They store all your passwords in an encrypted list, which you access with a single (ideally random and memorized) password, but they also have their own complications and compromises and haven't become standard equipment, yet. More often than not, I find they're banned by the powers in large corporate environments, who insist, "No. Thou Shalt Memorize Passwords." I would if I could, but I can't do more than a couple, and neither can anyone else, including the bonehead making that rule. Even when they're allowed, they work on only your own PC, which doesn't solve the problem of using your accounts on a public PC. You don't really want to be accessing your retirement account from one, but it would probably be reasonable to use one to check in for an airline flight.

Like an ancient Greek tragedy, the harder we struggle against it, the more firmly we get entangled. Being forced to secure each individual site in a different way leads to the overall result that none of them is secure at all. The number-one enemy of computer security isn't the packet sniffer (a machine that lets a guy, good or bad, view traffic on a computer network) that I discussed in Chapter 3; it's the Post-it Note. So what the heck can we do to make this software stop sucking?

OK, SO NOW WHAT?

Could we perhaps replace passwords with some other form of credential? In the case of a password, the authentication credential is something that you know, a secret that you and the system share. Alternatives could be something that you have, such as a key card, or something that you are, such as a fingerprint. These make a system more secure but are harder to use, so I don't see them entering the mainstream anytime soon. Here's why:

We could try authentication with a smart key or smart card, essentially a microchip containing a serial number. It's often packaged in the form of a credit card and plugged into a reader (see Figure 4–3); though they are now starting to appear in USB key

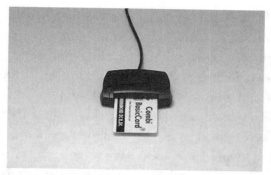

FIGURE 4-3 Smart card and reader

formats (see Figure 4–4). They cost about $20 each and you have to download and install software for each specific model. Instead of, or in addition to, asking you for a password, the site you're trying to log into asks your computer to read the card and send it the serial number, and if it's the one they're expecting from you, you're in. (I've left out all the cryptographic details that it uses to ensure no bad guy can steal it or fake it by watching the conversation.) The problem, obviously, is that the user has to physically have this device and the

FIGURE 4-4 SecuriKey smart card in a USB keychain form factor

server needs to know which device is associated with which user in order to authenticate. It works not too badly for long-term intimate situations, but it's death for casual, impulse-driven e-commerce. Can you imagine Amazon.com needing to send you a smart card and reader before you could order a book? And what would you do for other sites that would doubtless use different types of readers and cards? Think how your keychain and wallet are already clogged with supermarket and gas station and video store affinity cards; are you going to do this for each Web site you deal with? And how would it work on a computer that didn't have a card reader, such as a public computer in a library? You shouldn't be accessing your bank account from there, but a frequent flier account is probably reasonable. The casual, intermittent nature of most e-commerce means that this type of device isn't a good fit.

Smart cards today are useful primarily in conjunction with passwords in higher-security, ongoing relationship types of situations. For example, I need to connect my office computer over the Internet to the internal network of one of my clients because of some work I do for them. In addition to a user ID and password (which is random and which they make me change every few months) that company sent me a smart card and a reader. A bad guy cracking in from outside would not only have to steal a recognized smart card, but he'd also need to know the user ID and password associated with that card's user (which some users write on their cards, so they don't forget it; sigh). It's obviously more trouble than a user ID/password pair on its own. But access to this company's network is sensitive enough that they insist on it, and the work I do for them is lucrative enough that I put up with it. (Note: It doesn't protect them against me going crooked. The fear of what they would do to me does that.)

You will sometimes hear **biometric authentication** mentioned as if it were the Holy Grail. This term means authentication based on some immutable pattern of your body, such as a retinal pattern or fingerprint. It's often presented as the ultimate solution, because everyone automatically has her own individual fingerprints and you can't easily forget them. Early tests in supermarkets (Piggly Wiggly is the largest scale to date) seem to show that most customers like the idea. They register a credit card with the store and then simply touch their finger to the reader at checkout, sometimes keying in their home phone number as an additional layer of authentication. Senior citizens, in particular, enjoy not having to worry about losing their cash or cards, or having them stolen.

But apart from the problem of authenticating double-arm amputees (toe prints? nose prints? fake fingerprints?), fingerprint authentication is problematic because fingerprints are easy to steal and then can't be changed. Think—are you going to wipe off every glass you drink from in a restaurant? Every doorknob you turn? No way. When I make this point in a lecture, I emphasize it by taking the drinking glass out of the hand of the nearest person and holding it up to the light, highlighting the fingerprints on it. One of the beauties of passwords is that creating a new one is cheap, essentially free, so you can discard it anytime you think it might have been compromised. So I'm expecting a backlash against fingerprint readers once the bad guys start taking notice of them. For highly specialized situations requiring very tight security, such as Trident missile bases, a retinal pattern scanner probably makes sense. But if you can't imagine Amazon.com requiring a smart card reader to buy a book, how about imagining them requiring a retinal scanner. No password replacement here either.

Despite their shortcomings, we're stuck with passwords for the foreseeable future. What should users demand that developers do about it? Two things immediately. First, avoid them whenever possible. It ought to be possible to have a ten-minute stand with a Web site without promising eternal fidelity. (Note: Sometimes it isn't. For example, a mutual fund account is inherently a long-term, intimate relationship, which requires security all the way through at all times. So this paragraph won't apply to, say, Fidelity's and Vanguard's account maintenance Web sites.) For example, I just bought my three-year-old daughter a pair of her favorite pajamas over the Web. The store (to whom I won't give publicity because they annoyed me) required me to set up an online account, with a user ID and password, before they would sell them to me. I couldn't just type in my credit card number and delivery address, I had to set up an ongoing relationship. Can you imagine a brick-and-mortar store turning down your cash because you wouldn't give them ID? And this site was more annoying than usual. I had to try four times to choose a user ID that they would accept, refilling the entire form every time with my name and address, because they reset it. And their password rules wouldn't allow me to use the one I wanted either. If I hadn't been buying something that my daughter absolutely loves ("But Daddy, you *promised*"), I'd have told them to stuff it after the first failure, possibly before. Figure 4–5 shows a Web site that allows both.

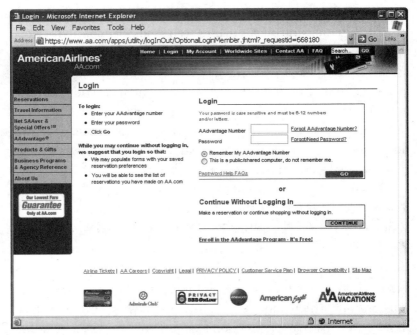

FIGURE 4-5 Web site allowing user to log in if desired, or to complete purchase without logging in

The most annoying misuse of authentication that I see today is online editions of newspapers, such as the *New York Times* and *Orlando Sentinel*. Even though access to these sites is free,[2] they insist on setting up accounts with user IDs and passwords and requiring these for access. They want to monitor their demographics, finding out which type of person reads which articles. Of course, they won't accept an e-mail address as an ID or symbolic characters in the password. They could track unique users with a simple cookie and not bother anyone, as does *Slate Magazine* and the Manchester, New Hampshire, *Union Leader*. Instead they're annoying you, annoying me, contributing to unchecked password proliferation and the heat death of the universe, and aren't even protecting anything. Naturally I lied on all the questions. The *Times* thinks I'm a 113-year-old (the maximum it would accept) woman living in Albania (the first choice on the country list). Their site designer is obviously ignorant of the Zeroth Law of Computer Science, which states simply, "Garbage In, Garbage Out." I hope you'll lie to them, too. Or use BugMeNot.com, a site which distributes login IDs contributed by other readers.

Second, developers should allow users a free choice of user ID and password. This means that the user must be able to use an e-mail address if she so desires, the rejection of which should be cause for a public flogging. A developer exists to make users' lives easier, not the other way around. And unless you are guarding a large sum of money such as a bank account, you ought to allow users to choose any password they want. Don't limit the choice of characters, and don't require strong ones. The users will only write them down, and then your password is as secure as a Post-it Note.

---

2. The *New York Times* recently started a service called Times Select, in which most of the paper's articles are free, but readers need a paid subscription to read their major columnists. Early returns indicate that customers are staying away in droves, and I'll bet you that the service will have imploded by the time you read this. The columnists, in particular, are annoyed at losing their large audiences, from which flow their influence and value.

LandsEnd.com does a fairly good job of adhering to both of these principles. When you check out from their Web site, you enter your shipping and payment information as usual, including your e-mail address for notification. The site then offers to remember your information, with your e-mail address as a user ID, if you just enter a password. Wisely, the password can contain any punctuation and symbolic characters (but doesn't require them), so it can be the same as your other Internet merchants if you like. You can easily understand what they're offering you, and accept it or not as you choose, with a minimum of extra work.

That's about the best anyone can do today, but authentication still has two major problems as it's currently practiced. First, not everyone does it this well—in fact, most companies don't, and those bozos spoil it for everyone else. Second, the Web is still very much in its infancy. It's the fastest-changing area of human endeavor that ever has existed. The current mechanisms for authentication have hit their limit. Think about the difficulty of entering a user ID and password on a smart phone using Triple-Tap Typing,[3] for example. If we want the Web to continue growing and evolving, we'll have to come up with a better mechanism for authentication than the shared secret password between user and server.

The problem of managing all these user ID/password pairs demonstrates a principal of software design called **scalability.** This means that a design approach that works well for a small number of users often stops working for inherent structural reasons when you try to apply it to a larger number. Suppose you wanted to design a telephone network, and you start by running wires directly from one house to another because it's easy. If you have only two houses, A and B, to connect, you need only one wire (see Figure 4–6a). A network

---

3. Triple-Tap Typing (TTT) is the way you key alphabetical characters into a numeric keypad device, such as a cell phone. When you press the "2" key once, you get the letter "A," press it again and you get "B," and so on. The difficulty of entering many names in this way accounts for the popularity of cell phones that can link up with your desktop PC address book.

for three houses requires three wires (A to B, A to C, and B to C), still pretty easy (see Figure 4–6b). A five-house network requires ten wires; now it's starting to get sticky (see Figure 4–6c). A ten-house network would require 45 wires, too many to install and manage. We say that the network design of running a separate wire from each house to every other house doesn't "scale up" beyond about four or five houses. At that point, we need a different design, probably one based on a central switching apparatus with one line from it to each house (see Figure 4–6d). Despite the cost of the switch, this would

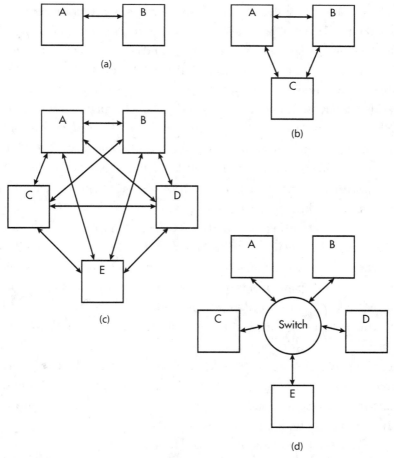

FIGURE 4-6 Scalability with (a) two houses; (b) three houses; (c) five houses, independent wires; and (d) five houses using central switch

be cheaper and easier to deal with than the ever-increasing number of wires. (A 100-house network would require 99 wires going into each house, for a total of 4,950 separate wires. I'll let you do the math on a 10,000-house town.)

The authentication design that we have today, with each Web site requiring its own credentials and performing its own authentication, doesn't scale well, for the reasons I've discussed. The user needs to maintain a separate set of credentials for each site, which I've already explained is annoying and inherently unsafe. Each site that does authentication needs to maintain its own record of users' credentials in such a way that the authentication program can read them when it needs to, but bad guys can't steal them. This represents a huge duplication of effort that's very expensive and difficult to do correctly.

The solution is something that we've already done in other areas of business. When my mother was a girl, consumer credit resided solely in individual credit accounts with specific merchants. When you bought meat, the butcher would add the cost to your bill, which you would pay at the end of the month. The baker would do the same thing. Almost nobody maintains individual credit accounts today. Instead, merchants have outsourced their entire payment process to credit card operators such as Visa and MasterCard, who handle the accounting, payment, and collection processes. The merchants get to concentrate on their core competency, selling clothes or fixing cars or whatever. The customer gets to establish a financial trust relationship with one or two or three credit card issuers, and have that relationship honored almost anywhere in the world. Neither side incurs the overhead of dealing with many bilateral relationships. The friction of the purchasing process is drastically reduced all around, as anyone knows who's recoiled in shock from a credit card bill. As they've outsourced payment, so Web sites should, nay, *must*, outsource their authentication to third parties, who a) know what they're doing and therefore b) do it properly.

That's not as crazy as it sounds. Think about it today in your non-computing life. For a few long-term, all-day, every-day relationships, you go to the trouble of getting a photo ID from that partner—your workplace, probably, or your school. Perhaps you get one for the supermarket you visit a couple of times each week. But you don't have a separate ID for each of the casual and occasional commercial interactions that require authentication. You don't have a separate UPS ID for picking up a package, or an airline ID for boarding a plane (different ones for each airline, naturally), or to prove your age for buying booze at Joe's Package Store, or to write a check almost anywhere. Having to create and maintain a separate relationship with every store that ever serves you alcohol would put a serious crimp in any holiday planning. Instead, you satisfy the authentication needs of all of these parties (are you the named addressee, were you born before a certain date) by presenting the government ID that you need to carry for driving a car or crossing a border. It's much easier for a vendor to accept this third-party credential than to insist on an intimate relationship with you. We've already outsourced authentication in most business relationships; it's now a matter of taking that concept onto the Web and making it work electronically.

The equivalent for computers is called **single sign-on.** A third party, called a **trust provider,** authenticates users for a fee. When you log into a Web site, instead of performing its own authentication, that site would pass your credentials to the trust provider, which would check them and tell the original Web site that it had authenticated you and was satisfied with your identity (see Figure 4–7). That way, you would use the same user ID and password at all participating sites, as you use your driver's license for identification at many different stores. It's an immensely powerful and scalable design. Despite the name, there probably wouldn't be just one trust provider; the free market would provide a choice of several, and merchants would decide which one or ones to affiliate with, as they now decide which credit cards to accept.

It'll be a while before we see this in production, however. Microsoft tried to do exactly this with its Passport system back

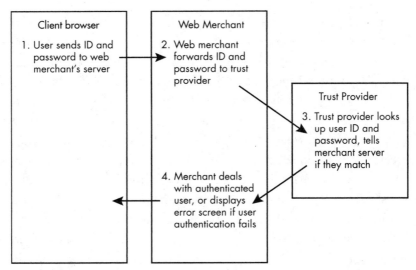

FIGURE 4-7 Single sign-on authentication, as implemented by Microsoft Passport

around 2000. If you've ever done anything with Microsoft online, such as MSN.com, Hotmail, or its Instant Messenger, you have a Microsoft Passport. It's a user ID (which is your e-mail address) and a password stored on a Microsoft Web farm. The original idea was that any Web merchant could outsource their customer identification to Microsoft for a fee. Microsoft hoped that many Web sites would choose this system, and life would be good.

At least it would have been. The problem is that almost nobody accepted Microsoft Passports for authentication except Microsoft itself. Passport's own Web site used to list only 84 sites that accepted it, of which 22 belong to Microsoft (plus Starbucks.com, which might as well belong to Microsoft because they drink so much of it). That's down from 90 the previous year, in a time of explosive growth of all things Internet. Now they won't even show you the list of merchants that accept it. As far as I can tell, Passport is now closed to new businesses, and eBay has dropped out as well. The market clearly rejected this particular implementation. (Spare me the outraged e-mails from the Passport team. Passport is a convenient standard for single sign-on among the manifold parts of Microsoft, and as such is fairly useful. As a universal Web standard, you swung and missed. Learn from it.)

The basic problem hindering the advance of Passport appears to be customers' willingness (or lack thereof) to allow Microsoft to hold their authentication data. I discussed Passport while teaching a class on .NET in a European country in September 2001. (Before.) I asked whether any of the students' companies had considered using Passport for basic authentication. Students representing three separate banks said that they had looked at it for their customer Web sites, but decided not to use it. The student with the best English explained, the others nodding agreement, that "As banks, the basic commodity we sell is trust. Would you trust your brother to hold your money? No [he must know my brother], but you trust us [he must *not* know my bank, whom I trust only because I owe them far more money in loans than they owe me in deposits]. We did research and focus groups, and found that an uncomfortable [he wouldn't quantify it] percentage of our customers would feel that we had betrayed their trust if we let Microsoft hold their authentication data instead of keeping it ourselves. They worry about it getting hacked, and they worry about it being used without their permission. I'm not necessarily saying that they're correct to worry about this, and I'm not necessarily saying that we're any better on our own, but like it or not, that *is* how our customers told us they feel. So if we don't want them to think that we've done to them the worst thing that a bank can do, betray their trust, we can't use it, and that's the end of that."

I won't bore you with them, but the technologies for implementing single sign-on exist today. Getting it to happen is more of a business question than a technical question. For example, who should the trust providers be? Not Microsoft, the market has already said. Probably not Sun or IBM either. Maybe banks, because we already trust them with our money, or maybe insurance companies, because we already trust their promise to pay if something bad happens to us. Maybe credit card issuers, because we sort of trust them and they're already on the hook for unauthorized purchases anyway. Maybe some form of government, because they're already in the authentication credential business, though we might not want to let them track us electronically. How will trust providers be paid, and by whom? How do we solve the chicken-and-egg problem of Web sites not using trust providers because no customers use them, but customers not using trust providers because no Web sites support them?

It will happen one day, and then online authentication will suck less than it does today. But for now

1. Security, particularly identity authentication, is a highly specialized field, of which an ordinary application programmer has no knowledge.
2. User IDs and passwords suffer from unchecked proliferation.
3. Boneheaded programmers (see point 1) exacerbate the proliferation problem (see point 2) because they often don't understand, or even realize that they need to understand, human factors (see point 3).
4. Outsourcing authentication to third parties is a great idea, and technically quite feasible, but no one has figured out the business model for it yet.

5
. . .

WHO'RE YOU LOOKING AT?

Online privacy touches a nerve in ordinary users. You've probably seen Peter Steiner's cartoon (Figure 5–1) before. It came out 84 dog years ago, many more when reckoned in Internet time. We chuckle and sigh wistfully over our naiveté in those early days, as we do over our children believing in Santa Claus or the Easter Bunny. No matter how much we wish we could return to that innocence, we know better. Although the Internet may seem anonymous, it really isn't. On the contrary, unless you've taken careful steps to cover your tracks, which almost no one does except bad guys, not only does your counterpart on the Internet know you're a dog, but they can easily find out your breed and age, whether you've had puppies, and how much you owe on your doghouse.

YES, THEY KNOW YOU

That scares and bothers a lot of people. While researching this book, I constantly found that privacy got more coverage in the nongeek press than any other computer-related issue, even security. The slant of the articles almost always is that Privacy (whatever the

"On the Internet, nobody knows you're a dog."

FIGURE 5-1 Ah, the innocence of our childhood years. (*Cartoon © The New Yorker Collection 1993, Peter Steiner from cartoonbank.com. All Rights Reserved.*)

term means) is a Good Thing, which means that revealing any information at all to anyone is a Bad Thing, because They (whoever that means) are watching you specifically, just dying to slather your most sensitive peccadilloes (say, flossing your teeth while watching Black Adder) across the front page of *USA Today*.

To some extent this worry is justified. You get angry when someone knows something about you that you feel they shouldn't. You'd go through the ceiling if your company's HR director read your medical claim forms and greeted you in the cafeteria line by saying, "Hi, Bob, how's the ol' leprosy today?" Or as columnist Adam Penenberg recently wrote on Slate.com: "…the illusion of privacy and anonymity allows our ids to slay our superegos. Let's not pretend that we haven't used the Internet to explore ideas we'd just as soon not share with friends, colleagues, family, or government prosecutors. Put another way: If you knew someone was looking over your shoulder when you Googled, would it change what you searched for?"

And yet, privacy, as with most things in the world, is a double-sided coin. You get almost as angry when someone doesn't know something about you that you think they should know. For example, when you call your bank or credit card company, they usually make you enter your account number from the keypad before starting the annoying phone menu.[1] And then when you finally get to a human, the first thing she asks for is your account number. *"I just keyed it in, for chrissakes!"* you scream at her. *"Why do you need it again, you lobotomized idoit?!"* Or the airline can't find your e-ticket, or can't credit the flight to your frequent flyer account. Or the emergency room doctor treating your child can't access your pediatrician's records to check her allergies. Or ... you get the idea.

People are all for privacy in the abstract until it makes their lives the tiniest bit more difficult, or someone offers them a dollar or two for giving up some of it. Then they'll fall over themselves handing over their data to warehouse clubs or frequent shopper programs. You laugh at the imagery, but how much trouble do you take so that the person who cleans your house or office can't read your confidential information? Do you bother shredding your bank statements so that your trash men can't steal them? Almost no one does. No matter what words come out of your mouth, your actions say that you find it more trouble than it's worth.

This chapter discusses the question of online privacy from the user's perspective. I'm talking about regular, ordinary users here, not wackos living in caves who only pay cash at the taxidermist so that no one can track them. (Guys, no one *wants* to track you.) And I won't address the question of privacy in the workplace, either. It's generally accepted that you have none whatsoever on the boss's nickel. I'll address the question of who knows what about when you

---

1. My father suggests that companies play messages when you're on hold that offer a chance for you to give feedback. "To say 'Damn you to hell,' press one. To say 'If my call is so bloody important to you, why don't you hire enough people to answer it, or do you think I'm too stupid to spot this lie,' press two. To say 'I'm coming to get you with a shotgun *right now*, you bastards!' press three." And so on.

use software packages or go online, how upset you ought to be about it, and what you can do to screw them up if you decide that you really care.

WHY IT SUCKS MORE THAN EVER TODAY

The ubiquity of the Internet, the fact that every intelligent box in the world is connected to every other box, affects every area of human endeavor. It's not surprising that it changes the privacy land-scape as well. Here are the main ways in which I see that happening.

The first is that data that has always been public is now much easier to get than it used to be, which means that many more people will look at it, think about it, and attempt to use it. For example, real estate transactions — this guy sold this house to that guy on such-and-such a date for this amount of money — have been public in my state for more than 300 years, but until the last five years or so, getting your hands on the data was very inconvenient. You had to drive to the Registry of Deeds during their limited business hours, find a place to park, walk to the building, wait in line while the unfirable patronage-appointed staff finished their coffee break, find the correct book if it was there, and so on. The sheer friction of the process meant that no one did it without a good reason. But now all registered deeds in Massachusetts are on the Web, so anyone can just pop up a browser in the comfort of his own office and bingo, there it is.

That sounds like a good idea, doesn't it? Public data is, by definition, public, so why shouldn't it be easy to get at? In researching this chapter, I looked up a college buddy of mine to see how much he had paid for his house in a nearby upscale town. I found the price in less than a minute at the Registry of Deeds Web site. But I also saw that his wife had originally bought the house in her own name a few months before they were married, and only put his name on the deed a few years later, around the time they had their second kid. Knowing his credit history as I do, that makes perfect sense (he still owes me money from 1977), but was it any of my business? Probably not, and I'm a little sorry now that I stuck my nose in. Since public information is now so much more easily available, many more people will know it and things like it. You'll have to keep your nose cleaner than you used to, and get better at ignoring other people's runny noses.

The second challenge to privacy in the modern computing environment comes from slicing and correlating existing data in new ways. For example, grocery stores have always kept track of how much of each item they sold in each week of the year in order to forecast demand patterns and keep their stores stocked. If they were really smart, they correlated total demand with external data such as the weather — order more ice cream if it's been unusually hot lately. But now, when you show them your affinity card to get their discounted prices, they record everything that you bought this week and tie it to what you bought last week and last month, a process known as **data mining.** (It's usually possible to tell them not to track this information, but you have to explicitly ask, a process known as **opting out.**) They might find that people who bought cat food also tended to buy large Thanksgiving turkeys a week early and bought red wine to go with it, whereas people who bought dog food waited until the last minute, bought smaller turkeys, and washed it down with white. They then might print individual coupons for you at checkout and adjust their inventories accordingly. ("Aha; a cat food guy: Print the large-turkey coupon and order more red wine.") With the razor-thin profit margins at most supermarkets, this type of intelligence could make the difference between staying in business and not. Doing this well is probably Wal-Mart's greatest strength.

Some people worry that the stores will somehow use this information to the customers' detriment. Others fear not so much the stores, but rather the government searching through the data that the stores have collected. For example, prosecutor Kenneth Starr attempted to subpoena Monica Lewinsky's bookstore purchase records, hoping they would illuminate her relationship with then-President Bill Clinton. The most agitating instance of that today is the Patriot Act, which allows the FBI to read a patron's library borrowing records without notifying the subject (with a search warrant granted by a judge, a fact that's often omitted from discussions of the act). I've offered my local library director a bumper sticker that says, "Fear the government that fears your library card."

The third major challenge to privacy is dealing with new types of data that haven't previously existed. For example, it's been easy for at least 15 years to get your instantaneous location on the Earth from a Global Positioning System satellite receiver, roughly the size of a paperback book and costing a few hundred dollars. The receivers have now gotten so much smaller and cheaper that they're often built into ordinary cell phones, such as the $80 Nextel i88s. The phone can transmit its current position over the wireless Web to a database, which any authorized person can then access over the Web. Companies can track their vehicles, parents can track their kids,[2] spouses can track their spouses. This type of information has only recently become available to ordinary people. How do we decide who's allowed to see which pieces of it, and under what circumstances?

Given the title of this book, you're probably expecting me to place all the blame on software developers. Unlike the other chapters, though, that wouldn't be true. Most of the computerized threat to privacy is not the result of boneheaded developers writing bad code because they don't understand their customers. Instead, it's the result of value-neutral software working more or less as intended, but employed by people whose values and interests run counter to yours. Like programmers, these marketingbozos (see Chapter 6) don't understand that you aren't like them, so they don't know what sorts of data collection you just shrug off and what sorts send you into paroxysms of rage. It's the same problem ("Know Thy User, for He Is Not Thee"), but in a different class of people.

---

2. See, for example, www.teenarrivealive.com

With some careful thought and a few small changes, however, the right software could really enhance users' privacy. To do this, though, geeks will have to do something they've never done before, which is understand their user and know that he's not like them. (Are you starting to see a pattern in this book?) The hopes and fears of programmers are very different from those of their users, and the privacy trade-offs that they would make are different as well. Simply writing software that says, "We let you take control of your privacy" would serve well only for users who actually do know which data is sensitive and which isn't, are willing to educate themselves about the options, and can deal with software to set them accordingly. That's essentially nobody in the world. Software for the common man recognizes that users don't know what's dangerous and what isn't, and provides reasonable default settings for reasonable users, right out of the box. Don't believe me? Here's an example.

USERS DON'T KNOW WHERE THE RISKS ARE

Tell me your bank account number—the checking account where your paycheck goes in, and comes out almost as quickly.[3] Go to this book's Web site, fill out the form, and e-mail it to me. And your bank's name and address, too, so I'll know exactly where to go to steal your money.

Don't want to do it, do you? Not just no, but "*Hell* no, Plattski! I don't trust you one tiny little bit, least of all with sensitive information like this. No way would I spill this sensitive information, and damn your eyes for even asking."

I can't say as I blame you. I wouldn't trust me either, not on the strength of a book like this. You shouldn't give out sensitive information like your bank account number. My local newspaper just ran a story about con men in the area, calling senior citizens

---

3. They say money talks, and it's true. I heard it once. It said, "Goodbye! So long, Plattski. It was a pleasure warming your wallet for a microsecond or two."

and pretending to be bank examiners, asking them for their account numbers to help catch criminals. Police advise you never to give out that information, which makes perfect sense. In fact, I'll advise you not even to type your credit card number into my Web site to buy this book. You should play it really, *really* safe, do things the old-fashioned way even if it takes a lot longer: Print out the paper form and mail me a personal check. That'll keep you safe, won't it?

Er, not exactly. What's written at the bottom of each and every check in your checkbook? Bingo, your account number and bank. They're even thoughtfully printed in magnetic ink so that I can scan them at high speed. I don't even have to worry about making a typing mistake. Oops.

And what's written on the top of most people's checks? Their address. Certainly you can order checks without them, but people who write a lot of checks generally put them there for convenience, because the merchants who accept checks require them. Sometimes they'll even print their drivers' license numbers on the check (those merchants again), and for many customers, that's their Social Security number as well. Double oops.

And now, to really win the bonehead prize, what's down at the lower right-hand corner of a check? That's right, the user authentication mechanism that's been used since the beginning of the written word: your signature, handwritten in ink. This used to be very hard to forge, requiring dexterity that almost no one had, and long years of practice even then. Now a simple $200 scanner can slurp it up and spit it out on a request to transfer money from your account to mine. Uh-oh.

You've always thought of checks as the safest way to transfer money, but that's not true anymore, is it? The checks themselves haven't changed, but the world in which they operate has. You live in that world, probably saw the changes happening, but never thought of their application to your ordinary checkbook. You can now see how difficult it is for ordinary users to know which pieces of information are sensitive and which aren't. It's further difficult for them to understand the various ways in which sensitive data can be spilled or stolen. And they shouldn't have to. They don't know what weather conditions are safe to fly in, that's why pilots make the decisions instead. They don't know which medications are safe for which diseases and with which interactions and side effects of other conditions, that's why doctors make those decisions instead. Why on Earth do people think they can know which information is safe to give out? They can't, they don't, and they shouldn't have to. Their software needs to do it for them; that's why they buy it.

WHAT THEY KNOW FIRST

Every computer on the Internet is identified by what's known as an **Internet Protocol (IP) address.** You can think of this as the computer's Internet telephone number (although it has nothing to do with the telephone number of the phone through which you've dialed in, if you still access the Web that way). A Web server has a fixed IP address, which means that it doesn't change from one day to the next, even if the server goes down and comes back up. Microsoft.com, for example, always occupies the IP address 207.46.130.108, and Amazon.com is always 207.171.166.102. If you type those numbers into your browser's address bar, you'll see that you get those sites. When you type in a human-readable address, such as "Microsoft.com", your browser actually looks up that name on another server (the "name server") to find the numeric address, then requests the site with that numeric address. (The status bars of some early browsers actually show you this lookup taking place.) That's like you saying "David Platt, Ipswich Massachusetts" into a voice phone, and having it look up my phone number and dial it for you.

When you're on the Internet, your computer also has an IP address, assigned to you by your Internet provider. This is known as a **dynamic IP address** because it isn't always the same from one browsing session to another. In the case of a dial-up modem, your provider assigns you the IP address when you dial in and recycles it when you hang up. It will probably assign it to another dial-up user before very long. A cable or DSL modem also gets assigned an IP address when it connects to the Internet provider and drops it when it disconnects. However, you often leave these sorts of connections permanently on, in which case it's not unusual to have the same IP address from one power failure to the next. If your cable modem is plugged into a backup power supply, you might have the same IP address for months or even years.

When you request a Web page, the site's server sees the IP address from which you are making the request, as caller ID on a voice phone displays the number of an incoming call. It has to, in order to know where to send the data you requested. You can see the current IP address of your computer by going to this book's Web site, selecting the Chapter 5 page, and following the IP Address Demonstration link. You'll see a page with your current IP address and some additional information I was able to find out about it.

Once the site has your IP address, it can look in various public databases to see which Internet provider owns that address. They're assigned to various providers by regulatory agencies, as telephone numbers are assigned to different telephone carriers. The geographic location from which your provider accesses the greater Internet is also usually public. So the Web site that you're accessing can usually quite easily figure out the country from which your request originates. The next time you go to a Web site that makes you select the country from which you're requesting (UPS.com, Guinness.com), know that they're too lazy or too stupid to pick the country off your incoming IP address, and are making you do the work instead. If you've read Chapter 2 yet, you probably remember me lambasting UPS.com for failing to use this technique. Send them mail telling them so, won't you? And then take your business to a company that cares about your convenience (easy with UPS, harder with Guinness).

Your Internet provider usually maintains a log file of which IP address it has assigned to which user at any given moment. So if you use an Internet account that's assigned to you, the server can probably find out exactly who you are without much trouble. While most providers say they won't match it to your identity, their policies usually contain loopholes for court-ordered disclosure, and for violating the provider's acceptable use policies. They probably won't do it as long as you behave yourself. But if someone traces spam or other attacks to a provider's IP address, they'll track it back to your computer.

If you don't like that idea, it's not hard to keep a site from tracking you down. You can use a public PC, such as at a library or a Kinko's store (make sure you pay with cash, and steer clear of the security cameras or wear a disguise), the Internet equivalent of a pay phone. Or you can use an anonymizer service, as I'll describe later in this chapter, which makes it seem like you're coming from a different IP address. Few people bother. Most like the idea of their Internet provider policing their area of the Web more than they dislike it—to the extent that they think about it at all, which isn't much or often.

MILK YOU WITH COOKIES?

The culprit in many Web privacy violations is the misuse of a thing called a **cookie**. Much heat and not much light have appeared in the press over cookies, and many people are confused about exactly what they are and how they work. "They're Good!" one article yells. "They're Bad!" screams another. "Cookies don't track people, people track people." "Yeah, people track people *with cookies*, you moron." Lighten up, everybody. Cookies are not inherently evil; indeed, they are necessary to get the Web experience that most users demand. But they can also be used to do things that you might not want. Here's how.

As I explained in Chapter 2, in the beginning of the Web, all of its pages were static. By this I mean that their content was the same for all users at all times, and did not depend on any information that the user provided. The Web page author sat down and wrote out, say, a list of the movies playing at the local cinema, and that's what you saw when you viewed that page in your browser. If this is all Web pages ever did, then there would be no need for cookies.

The problem occurs when we want to tailor a Web page's content according to the preferences of a particular user. Suppose, for example, that you type www.cnn.com into your browser's address bar, requesting the home page of that major news provider. CNN has both a U.S. edition and an international edition of its home page, the contents of which are different. (Try them and see.) CNN's server detects from your IP address (see previous section) the country from which you are probably making the request, and it shows you that country's edition first. However, the IP address location might be wrong, or you might be on the road and homesick, or you might just be interested in the other edition's viewpoint. CNN therefore provides a link near the top of the page to change it (see Figures 5–2a and 5–2b, upper right corner).

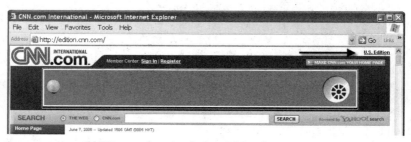

FIGURE 5-2a CNN.com showing link to U.S. edition

FIGURE 5-2b CNN.com showing link to international edition

Now, suppose you're looking at CNN.com's home page and you click on a link to jump to some article. How can the server know which edition of the home page you were looking at, and therefore which formatting (U.S. or international) to apply to the new page? A Web page request doesn't automatically contain this information, because no one cared about this sort of thing when the request protocol was designed many years ago. The connection between your browser and the server disappears after each page request, by design, a condition that programmers call **stateless.** It isn't like a phone line where you stay connected until you hang up. The server doesn't know which user the new request is coming from. (IP address tracking isn't sufficient because the owner of the incoming address could have changed from one request to another, and because connection-sharing arrangements often make the requests of several computers appear as though they're coming from the same IP address.)

To provide you with the appearance of a connected conversation, Web programmers need to somehow remember information from your first Web page request and make it available to the server on your next request, whenever that is. They do this by means of a cookie, a small text file that lives on your computer's hard disk or sometimes in your browser's memory. When you select the U.S. or international edition, the CNN.com server writes this information into CNN.com's cookie (creating it if it doesn't already exist) on your machine. The next time you request a page from CNN.com, the server reads your edition choice information from this cookie and uses it to format the page accordingly. Many other personalization features can be stored in the cookie—for example, the language in which to display the Web page.

Each Web site has its own cookie on your machine. A Web site server can read only the cookies it has placed there itself. The browser doesn't allow it to read other ones, and failure to enforce this restriction is a bug in the browser. So Amazon.com can't see what you did at BarnesAndNoble.com, and Guinness.com can't see what your settings are for Budweiser.com. Cookies aren't large, usually only a few hundred characters each. If you search your disk for the term *cookies* you'll probably see a folder full of them, as shown in Figure 5–3. Cookies can't hurt your machine. They're simple text files, not programs; they cannot run. They exist only to contain information placed on your disk by a particular server.

Cookies are often used to remember the ID of a logged-in user, which many users find convenient on low-security sites. For example, many newspaper sites, such as the *New York Times*, require you to enter an ID and password to read most of their content. You can, however, tell it to remember your identity so that you don't have to enter it every time. The *Times'* Web server does that by placing your ID into its cookie. It doesn't store your password there, but it does store a special value that says it has checked your password and found it valid. Sites which remember a lot of information about you—for example, your lifetime buying history on Amazon.com—don't store it in the cookie. They store it in their own internal databases and use the cookie only for storing your ID, which they then use to look you up in the databases.

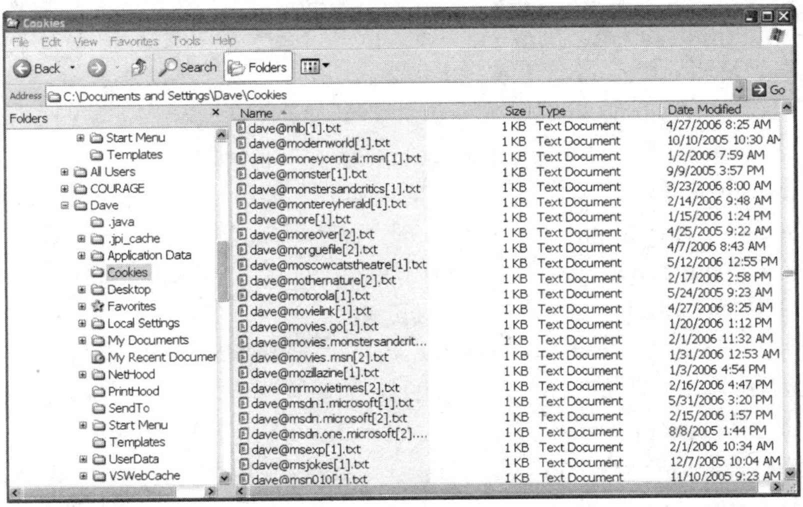

FIGURE 5-3 Cookie folder

Cookies help not only users, but also site designers and administrators. For example, they allow a site designer to track an individual user's path through the site, even though the designer doesn't know the user's real-world identity—whoever-it-is started at this page, then she went to that page, then she left our site and went somewhere else. Fifty other people did the same thing, but ten went on from that second page to another page of ours. Perhaps the second page needs more links to other useful content to encourage users to stay on the site, or a better layout so that users can see the links that do exist.

Cookies are also useful for advertising. They can remember which ads you've been shown and which ads you've clicked on, allowing the site to better select the ads it shows you. For example, if you've recently clicked on an ad about boats, the site might show you more boat-related ads and fewer about golf. Or perhaps they'll discover that people who like boats also buy more booze than the average customer (to drink on the boat, I guess), so they'll show you more booze ads because you clicked on a boat ad. Sites generally get paid for an ad only when a user clicks it, not for merely showing it. For sites that are advertiser supported, as is CNN, maximizing the click-through rates is a life-or-death problem. Stores that customize their home pages based on a user's previous purchases, such as Amazon.com showing your latest recommendations, also depend on this technique.

You can now see how sites depend on cookies for the customization that users insist on, and for commercial purposes that keep them alive. You'd think that a symbiotic relationship like this would please both parties. So what's all the fuss about cookies, because believe me, there's plenty. Well, some users, on principle, don't want to give any Web site any information at all. "None of your damn business, shut up, don't ask," they say. Others hate all ads, so they don't want to give any information that would make them more effective. (These users often buy utilities such as AdSubtract and GhostSurf, which remove banner ads entirely, leaving only blank spaces on the screen.) Some users feel that they've been trespassed on because that sneaky server wrote something on their machine without asking. I'm sorry, but the stateless nature of the Web connection makes technical alternatives difficult and expensive.

The bad privacy problem arises when a site ties a user's surfing habits to a real-life person. You can use a false identity at most newspaper sites, and I suggest in Chapter 4 that you do that just for spite. But a site where you actually purchase things, such as Amazon.com or an airline site, needs to authenticate your real-world identity to verify your payment transactions. A fair number of people are worried that this information will somehow wind up somewhere that it shouldn't. Most of them worry for about five seconds, try it once, see that nothing bad happens to them, and then get on with their lives. But it could backfire sometime in the future. For example, the next time you're nominated for cabinet secretary, what if a reporter digs up your surfing history—"On Amazon.com in 2005, you searched 17 times for books on torture, even though you didn't buy any. What were you looking for?" Amazon's privacy statement (see the next section of this chapter) says they won't give this information away, but I have a hard time believing that would hold up against an ambitious reporter smelling a scoop and a self-righteous database administrator who didn't like your politics. If this is a problem for you, either try one of the anonymizer products I discuss later in this chapter, or drive to the brick-and-mortar bookstore and pay cash, or start thinking of a good alibi. ("I was diligently searching for what *not* to do!")

This problem becomes especially acute when sites start to pool their data. That's what DoubleClick.com did back in 1999 and 2000. You may remember that kerfuffle; it made the evening news in a way that software matters seldom do.

Many Web sites don't manage their own advertising, because it's expensive and difficult. Instead, they allow agencies such as DoubleClick.com to sell ads to businesses, serve them up online, keep track of which ads work for which user, and send them a check for the clicks at the end of the month. The privacy policies of sites as diverse as PizzaHut.com, Travelocity.com, and Shoeline.com all list DoubleClick as their advertising partner, and DoubleClick claims that so do more than 11,000 other sites.

The problem erupted when DoubleClick started pooling data from all the Web sites for which it served ads. They played a rather sneaky trick that let them put a single cookie on a user's machine and then access that cookie from any Web site that served up a DoubleClick ad.[4] This would allow them, if they wanted, to know that the guy looking at shoes on Shoeline.com had just bought a trip to Hawaii at Travelocity, so perhaps they'd show him ads for sandals rather than mukluks. (DoubleClick claims they don't currently record that level of customer detail, going down only to the level of market sector—for example, sports, pets, travel, etc.)

This was too much sharing for many users. Some filed lawsuits against it, which the company won, the court deciding that the users had not proven they had been damaged by the data pooling. Their concern was amplified because DoubleClick had just acquired a major marketing data company called Abacus, which owned a huge database of mail order consumer records. DoubleClick threatened, nay, promised its customers, to combine that data with cookie data and make a personally identifiable Web surfing record across every site for which it served an ad. Even though they won the eventual lawsuit, the controversy hammered DoubleClick's stock price and they backed down. For now, anyway.

As with most things in life, cookies are double-edged. I spend a hell of a lot of money at Amazon.com. I'd be very annoyed if a human at a store where I spent that amount of money didn't remember who I was or some notion of what I liked. On the other

---

4. The Web site would place a tiny image, often just one dot, on each page of their site. This image, known as a **web beacon,** was marked as coming from DoubleClick.com. When the browser assembled the page to show to the user, it would request that image from DoubleClick.com. This would allow DoubleClick's server to see its own cookie, regardless of the page the user had requested. This trick is known as a **third-party cookie.**

hand, even a technophile like me can see the problem of a person-ally identifiable Web surfing record available to anyone with $20. I occasionally wonder what my old college buddy, the one whose real estate transaction I snooped on, has been looking at lately, and I'd be delighted to pay $20 for the chance to embarrass him at our next class reunion.

Most browsers allow you some control over the cookies on your system. Until recently, this control was too lame to be useful. You could turn cookies off completely, but then you'd find that many convenient Web site features will not work. Typing in your user ID and password every day to read the *New York Times*, and the *Orlando Sentinel*, and the *Washington Post*, and so on and so on, gets very old, very quickly, when you know that relief is just a check-box away. Other sites, such as the popular free e-mail services of Hotmail and Yahoo!, won't work at all without cookies. You could set your browser to prompt you before allowing each cookie, but then you would have to stop and think and click OK or Cancel three or four times before viewing every single page. That gets very old in about five seconds. I can't imagine who thought this type of feature would be useful to anyone.

The control situation is getting a little better. Internet Explorer version 6 allows you more fire-and-forget control, as shown in Figure 5–4. It accepts some types of cookies and blocks others, but I was never able to figure out exactly what it meant by "third party cookies that use personally identifiable information without your implicit consent." The browser doesn't say, and tracking it down somewhere is more work than I'm willing to do. You can slide the control up or down to make it somewhat tighter or looser. You can also set it to block all cookies and then add exceptions—no cookies except for Google.com, say, or Google.com and Amazon.com. I've chosen a hybrid. If you click on the Advanced box, which no ordi-nary user ever does, you see the box shown in Figure 5–5. I select Accept for first-party cookies (the site I'm actually looking at) and

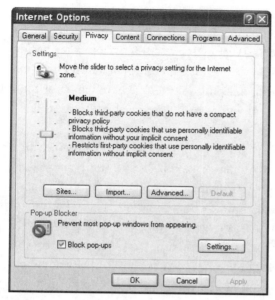

FIGURE 5-4 Default privacy settings in Internet Explorer 6. Can anyone figure out what these cookie settings mean? I can't.

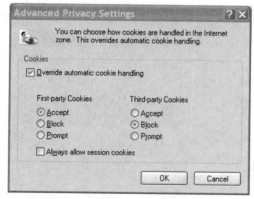

FIGURE 5-5 My custom cookie-handling setting in Internet Explorer 6

Block for third-party cookies (the trick that DoubleClick uses). So far, I'm happy with that setting.

PRIVACY POLICY NONSENSE

Every Web site that collects personal data contains a privacy policy. Unfortunately, they're so full of legalistic claptrap that I find it impossible to get any useful information from them. There's an enormous supply of this dreck, so someone somewhere must be demanding it, but I'll be damned if I know who.

In researching this chapter, I went to HarryPotter.com, which is owned by Warner Bros. Their privacy policy contains more than 2,100 words, 400 more than the introduction to this book. And it's a lot less enjoyable, I assure you. It doesn't contain any jokes, except maybe where they say, "Your privacy is important to us." Microsoft Word's grammar checker puts its reading level at about twelfth grade, roughly equivalent to the *Wall Street Journal*. (Most newspapers are written at an eighth-grade level, and this chapter is about ninth grade.) Considering that the Harry Potter series of books is targeted at fifth graders, a twelfth-grade reading level is pretty high for communicating something you want your readers to understand.

It starts with the usual corporate platitudes. As far as I can tell from the legalese, it comes down to: "We do what the hell we want. If you don't like it, tough." There's very little in the way of laws, almost nothing in the U.S. and not much more in the rest of the world, that govern what they're permitted to do with it.[5] Only the free market does that. You more or less trust that Warner Bros. isn't going to do anything awful with your information. And they probably won't. They're a mass-market consumer corporation. The fear of losing their carefully cultivated warm, fuzzy image probably protects your privacy more effectively than any law.

Besides, it doesn't matter what the privacy statement says when you give them your information. At the end of it is the all-purpose disclaimer that says they can change it at any moment—

---

5. The main exception to this is in the health care industry, where laws such as HIPAA are draconian and very confusing. Because of its specialized nature, I won't discuss that case.

"From time to time, we may update this privacy notice. We will notify you about material changes in the way we treat personally identifiable information by placing a notice on our site. We encourage you to periodically check back and review this policy so that you always will know what information we collect, how we use it, and to whom we disclose it." Translation: "We might change this. Don't like that? Tough." Eight words rather than 63. In the unlikely event that you wade through this morass once, will you ever, *ever* do it again? And with every one of the dozens, if not hundreds of sites you deal with? No way. So anything can change and you'd never know it. That's what watchdog privacy agencies are for, to sound the alarm when a com-·pany steps out of bounds and tries to rally the market against it. I think, however, they'd be more effective if they didn't cry wolf as often. See what I say about Google's Gmail service later in this chapter.

Microsoft is much better than Warner Bros. on the question of changes to the privacy statement. The privacy statement for their Passport authentication service (see Chapter 4) says that ".NET Passport will obtain your opt-in consent for any updates to this Privacy Statement that materially expand the sharing or use of your personal information in ways not disclosed in this Privacy Statement at the time of collection." That's about the best you could hope for. Passport has failed in the market, though, and isn't used in very many places.

Strangely enough, the worst offender of the cookie universe has one of the best and most detailed privacy policies on the Web. DoubleClick.com's privacy statement contains no fewer than 30 separate subpages. It explains exactly how they do the third-party cookie placement, what the cookie is made up of, the types of site visits that it logs, and how to opt out so that it won't collect data about you. It explains exactly what it was trying to do in connecting your surfing history to the name and address database that it got from Abacus. It promises that they won't do it, and it contains an excerpt from a Federal Trade Commission letter saying they believe DoubleClick's assurances that they aren't doing it. You may or may not think this is sufficient, and you may or may not believe they'll actually do what they say they'll do. But they spell it out in more exacting detail than anyone else I've seen.

Here's the privacy statement that I use on my programmer newsletter: "Thunderclap does not accept advertising; nor do we sell, rent, or give away our subscriber list. We will make every effort to keep the names of subscribers private; however, if served with a court order, we will sing like a whole flock of canaries. If this bothers you, don't subscribe; instead, just read the newsletter online." I'd say that sums it up for most sites. They could do with fewer words to say it, though.

COVERING YOUR TRACKS

There are times and places in which someone really needs to be anonymous online. The classic example is blowing the whistle on illegal activities by governments. Given all that we've seen, is anonymity even possible? It depends on who you're hiding from and how hard you're willing to work at it.

It's fairly easy to send anonymous e-mail through an **anonymous remailer.** This is a server, usually run by an ideological volunteer, which accepts mail from anyone and forwards it to the recipient without disclosing the identity of the sender. The recipient sees that it came from the anonymous remailer, but has no information beyond that. The remailer operator keeps no records (or at least claims to keep no records) of which message came from which source. Obviously that makes replying somewhat problematic, but this type of message often requires none — "here's a leak; publish it." The location and operation of anonymous remailers change frequently, so I can't easily point you at a good one. And how would you know which one to trust, anyway? Try the public library or Kinko's route. Or just burn the data on a CD and drop it in the snail-mail box.

If you don't want a Web site to know the IP address you're coming from, it's not hard to obscure yourself. A number of products exist that will cover your tracks for a fee, such as Anonymizer from Anonymizer Inc. and GhostSurf from Tenebril Inc. When you type, say, CNN.com into your browser, the request doesn't get sent to CNN.com. Instead, it goes to Anonymizer's server computer, which then requests CNN.com's page and returns the results to you. CNN's server sees the request as coming from Anonymizer's IP address rather than yours. Now it's a game of check and countercheck, as some Web sites refuse requests from known anonymizers, figuring they won't get many ad clicks from someone who's taken their time and effort to cover their tracks. How safe is it? It depends how much you trust the anonymizer service to keep the data private. Against the National Security Agency? Probably not. Against your boss at work? Probably. (Unless, of course, you work for the NSA.)

Most users don't want to take the trouble to do this. Going through an anonymizer is usually slower than connecting directly, because you're making two network hops rather than one. Occasionally it'll mess up other applications. Most users don't care whether a Web site can figure out that they're coming from, say, the Boston area. A lot of times they'd even prefer it so that searching for, say, a dentist can provide one in their local area. The Internet gets used for an awful lot of mundane, boring stuff that no one cares about snooping on. It's very hard to pick the juicy nuggets out of all that background noise, and most users are comfortable with that position.

THE GOOGLE CONUNDRUM

You can see the trade-offs of privacy versus service in Google's popular Gmail service (see gmail.google.com). I find it interesting that very few people perceive it as a dilemma. Every single person I've spoken with about it has had a powerful gut reaction, saying either "Wow! Cool! I want one, where do I get it?" or "Yuck! Awful! Those guys should be shot for even thinking about it."

On April 1, 2004, the Web search firm Google announced a new, free Web-based e-mail service called Gmail, similar to those of Hotmail and Yahoo!. Google offered a much larger mailbox than the others — 1,000 megabytes (about one-and-a-half compact discs' worth), as opposed to two megabytes for Hotmail and four for Yahoo!. Some users were skeptical because of the announcement date, but it turned out to be real after all.

All three Web-based mail services are supported by advertising. The difference, and the catch, if you consider it that, is that Gmail chooses ads based on the content of each e-mail message as you read it. Its computers scan the message as they format it for your display and select ads based on the keywords they find in the message. It's conceptually similar to the way Google's Web search site shows you ads based on the words in your search request. As with the search site, the ads are text based and sit quietly off to the side. You can see an example in Figure 5–6. The message deals with cell phones, so the ads do as well. Figure 5–7 shows the same message in Yahoo!, which selects ads based on your demographic profile (age, gender, etc.). You can see that it has a generic restaurant advertisement across the top and ads for credit cards and horoscopes down the left-hand side. The ads are graphical and often flash or dance around in a way I find quite annoying.

Some people hate the idea of Gmail scanning messages for ads. Thirty-one privacy organizations signed a letter to Google within a week of the announcement, urging them not to do that, saying in part that "the scanning of confidential e-mail violates the implicit trust of an e-mail service provider." One California state legislator (to whom I won't give the publicity of mentioning her name, for being such an annoying bluenose) went so far as to file legislation to forbid it, which didn't pass. Articles with balanced and unsensational titles such as "Datapocalypse" described it as "the

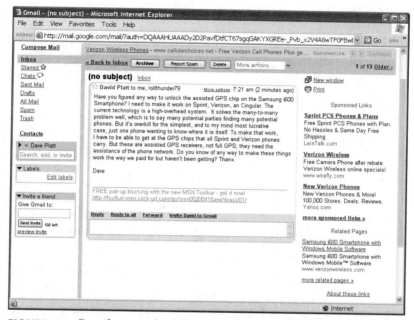

FIGURE 5-6 Gmail screen displaying context-sensitive ads

FIGURE 5-7 Yahoo! Mail screen for same message

beginning of a new information surveillance regime."[6] The altercation was bigger than the one I remember over fluoridated water in my original hometown in the Pennsylvania coal country.

On the other hand, most non-privacy-fundamentalist users I spoke to don't give a flying fish that Google's reading their mail to choose which ads to show them. If anything, they're happy the ads are potentially more useful because they're tightly targeted.[7] If I'm having a mail conversation with someone about painful hemorrhoids and an ad for a new remedy comes up, I might be very grateful, and it won't happen on Hotmail. These users figure that spam filters already scan their messages anyway, for which they are very glad, and most people's work e-mail accounts are monitored by their employers. They don't have any serious expectation of privacy on their e-mail accounts, especially the free Web-based ones. If they ever give a damn about securing a particular piece of e-mail, they'll encrypt it with Pretty Good Privacy or another tool, but they almost never do. They also find Google's text ads less obtrusive than the distracting graphics on the other services. I count myself in this group and say to the fundamentalists who want to forbid consenting adults from choosing this service, "Hey, we're grownups. If we want you to save us from ourselves, we'll ask you to. Besides, Google offers a triple-your-money-back guarantee if you're not completely satisfied." (Remember, it's a free service.)

---

6. Annalee Newitz, writing in Metroactive.com, May 5 through 11, 2004.

7. In fact, Google's context sensitivity can be a source of endless amusement, at least to geeks. I know a pair of them that have a case of good beer riding on who can be the first to send a message through Gmail that brings up an ad mentioning the book or movie *Silence of the Lambs*. To make it sporting, they've agreed the message can't mention the title, the names of the main characters, the actors who played them in the movie, or the book's author. (Do you want to say "Get a life," or do you want me to?) I'll post the winner on the book's Web site if and when there is one. I expect this sport to spread faster than the pet rock craze, with online tournaments, commercial sponsorships; all leading up to the world championships, sponsored of course by Google. To coin another word, I've called this new sport Googleplexing™, and have reserved the Web address Googleplexing.com as the world headquarters for the interested community.

Google's competitors are already responding. Yahoo! has increased the size of its free mailbox to 250 megabytes. Hotmail is selling a 2,000 megabyte account, twice the size of Gmail's free one, for only $20 per year, with no ads at all. Having more choices is a Very Good Thing. Customers have many choices: Would they prefer to watch tailored text ads or random graphical ones, or pay cash to watch none at all? Google in return has raised the size of its mailbox from 1,000 megabytes to 2,500. The free market, as it should and as it always does, will determine whether Gmail will succeed. I think it probably will because most users trust Google. But I doubt that Microsoft could get away with a plan like this.

SOLUTION

Privacy is a funny beast. As we've seen in this chapter, privacy means many things to many people. And not all privacy problems spring from badly written or malicious software.

The solution is partly legislative. New technological capabilities will require new types of regulation. We didn't need a law against talking on cell phones while driving until we had cell phones. As computers become more powerful and more connected, they'll need regulation to keep them from being used for evil rather than good. For example, the Video Privacy Protection Act (18 U.S.C. § 2710), making it a crime to disclose a customer's video rental records, was passed in response to the disclosure of Robert Bork's video records during his 1988 Supreme Court confirmation hearings (which he failed). Making it a crime to view someone's tax or medical records without consent would be a good place to start. You can't depend on users taking action, though. They don't know what to do or where to look, and they're already confused by the technology. The European Union has stronger laws on data privacy than the U.S., usually requiring opt-in consent to collect and use data, but the opt-in boxes are often checked by default and buried in the licensing agreements where no one ever sees them.

Part of the solution is technical. You can use programs such as anonymizers and ad blockers to increase your privacy and limit the amount of information collected. They'll improve, I'm sure. They don't cost much, but sometimes cause compatibility problems with other programs. My ad blocker is fighting with my virus scanner as I write these words. Knock it off, you two, or I'll punish you both. If nothing else, tools will allow you to be more private than your neighbor, because most people won't lift a finger.

Part of it's simply being on your toes. It's usually easy to opt out of any information collection. Most vendors would rather not have you around if you're not interested. It costs them money to have you, and might cost them a lot more if you cause trouble.

The current online privacy landscape reflects the capitalist free market, as does almost everything. You have market research companies busily collecting data, trying to make a buck by slicing and dicing it in interesting ways. You have watchdog agencies ready to scream at any perceived invasion, justified or not. And you have the masses, Richard Nixon's "silent majority," in the middle, trying to get their work done and raise their children and have a little fun, without a whole lot of extra time and energy to worry about icky raisins in their online cookies. To the extent that they do think about it, they look for a quick fix—buy this tool, install it, and stop worrying. If they perceive a serious threat, they'll scream, as they did in 1998 when national drugstore chain CVS sent out marketing letters to its pharmacy customers, based on their medical records. And mass-market companies will cave at the first sight of anything resembling organized resistance.

To my mind, the best way to throw a monkey wrench into the privacy snoopers is also the easiest and the most enjoyable. I speak, of course, of deliberate obfuscation. Don't refuse to give them data. Instead, give them bad data. Lower the signal-to-noise ratio of the data they collect until it's not profitable anymore. For example, Babies 'R Us asked for my ZIP Code when I bought diapers the other day in Massachusetts. Instead of telling them to buzz off, I made one up from California. Swap grocery store affinity cards with your neighbors—the store will see a person buying cat food, organic alfalfa sprouts, and Pampers one week; dog food, cigarettes, and Depends the next. Even more amusing than the thought of the Gallup/Zogby presidential election exit poll returning a 100 percent response for "Get out of my face, turkey, 'fore I smack you upside the head," is the thought of them calling it the wrong way and looking really stupid. When a political pollster calls me, I don't hang up; I take the time and effort to lie to him. I lie deliberately and with malice aforethought. And I enjoy doing it, very much. I always wonder whether the marketingbozo writing down my answers wonders why I'm chuckling. So join me. It doesn't take more than a few percent, and at the next election we'll have the funniest night of political idiocy since Henry Kissinger got the Nobel Peace Prize.

I'd normally end the chapter here and let that be the last word. But a reader commenting on an early draft of this chapter wrote to me, "I don't really care about cookies and other stuff. It doesn't cost me anything. The real thing I fear is identity theft and one day waking up to an empty bank account." As I read those words, I realized that this reader had his priorities straight, unlike so few others on either side of the privacy arguments. So now that you know where the privacy problems lie, you know enough to realize that they rank much lower than your security worries. Go back and reread the security chapter, then take the actions that it tells you to take. Only when you're finished with that should you devote even a single minute to worrying about whether the shoe store site knows you've visited a travel site recently.

6

. . .

TEN THOUSAND GEEKS, CRAZED ON JOLT COLA

You can tell a lot about an animal by studying it in its native habitat. If you want to know about the geeks who produce the software you use (and don't like), then come with me now. I'll take you to one of their major conferences and show you what they're like when they think there's no one else watching.

SEE THEM IN THEIR NATIVE HABITAT

There are many, many computer conferences throughout the year, on all sorts of topics. I could probably do nothing but go around speaking at one after another if I wanted to (except I wouldn't make much money and I'd soon collapse from exhaustion). They range in size from 20 people up to the largest of all, Microsoft's Tech Ed. To show the greatest diversity of geek behavior and by extension the greatest unanimity where it isn't diverse that's where I'll take you.

Tech Ed is an annual series of conferences, usually starting in late May or early June and going through the summer. I've been speaking at them on and off since 1999, and I've gotten to really like them. One is held in the United States, another one in Europe, and several others throughout the Asia/Pacific area. The U.S. incarnation, where we're about to go, draws about 10,000 attendees, so it can be held only in cities with the largest convention centers. Dallas. Las Vegas. New Orleans. Orlando. My nearby hometown of Boston just built a new convention center, so I'm looking forward to sleeping in my own bed when they hold it here in 2006.

ALL THESE GEEKS

Getting 10,000 geeks into the same building and maintaining them all week without killing anyone is quite a logistical challenge. You might think that the basic input and output requirements of food and toilets would be the biggest stumbling blocks, but the conference centers generally have those figured out. Instead, the biggest challenge is providing Internet connectivity. Geeks need their Internet; for e-mail, for instant messenger, for browsing about the interesting things they're learning. A geek without Internet access is like a heroin addict without a fix. They're jumpy, they sweat, they bounce off the walls, they drool.

To solve the connectivity problem Tech Ed has more than 1,000 PCs set up in a hall for attendees to use. The scale boggles you when you first see it, row upon row, like the identical headstones in a veteran's cemetery (see Figure 6–1). The geeks stream to it at every break; dashing by even tables piled high with Krispy Kreme donuts. Perhaps, being geeks, they figure that with a pile that high, there are sure to be some left when they finish their e-mail, and they're usually right. Counterintuitively, a smaller pile might cause them to stop.

FIGURE 6-1 Tech Ed PC room, empty

In addition to the wired PCs, the airwaves at the conference crackle with geek wireless communication devices. The entire building contains wireless Ethernet for notebook PCs, similar to that found in your local Starbucks but a thousand times the size. Geeks bring their own gadgets, as much to show them off to other geeks as to get any work done with them. High-speed cellular modems in a notebook PC for when you're out of the Internet hot spot. Palmtop PCs with built-in cell phones. Cell phones with built-in palmtop PCs. Cell phones and palmtops with wireless earpieces using a low-powered radio technology called Bluetooth. I keep waiting for someone to pull out Maxwell Smart's shoe phone from the old TV series, *Get Smart*.

Everyone wears a dorky badge holder around his neck proclaiming his name and company. It's a great starter of conversations or fistfights: "Borland, eh? Didn't they used to be a software company or something?"[1] I struck up a conversation with one of the few female attendees when I noticed that her badge said she was from the Monterey Bay Aquarium Research Institute, the research arm of my daughters' all-time favorite destination. I offered to stop in and give a talk the next time I passed by. That'll let me write off my travel, and maybe they'll let my daughters meet an otter.

Unlike conventions of, say, surgeons, everyone at Tech Ed wears T-shirts, and these are great conversation starters as well. I rode an escalator with a guy wearing one from Live365.com, a Web site where anyone can program a musical show and legally stream it out to listeners. I've wondered how it worked since I acquired a taste for some of their beach music streams, and the guy explained it all on the ride up. You wouldn't do that with some random stranger on the street, but here in the conference center it's OK. Like a church (and in some ways Tech Ed is a church, the Holy Mother Church of Geekery), the roof is the only introduction you need.

In addition to their habits of dress and communication, geeks have a peculiar pattern of eating and drinking. Their consumption of caffeine is already legendary. I know I'm falling into the conference routine when I move the hotel coffee maker next to my bed so that I don't have to get out, to start it in the morning. The breaks between talks feature drums of coffee, espresso carts with long lines, and bins of the geek favorites Mountain Dew and Jolt Cola ("All the sugar, and twice the caffeine!"). I first discovered caffeinated water

---

1. Borland was a major player in the early days of PCs, one of the brightest rising stars in the '80s and early '90s. Their cheap ($50) and excellent (by the standards of its time) Turbo Pascal introduced many newcomers to programming. Their willingness to offer software products with a 30-day money-back guarantee and without copy protection forced other vendors to do the same. Unfortunately, through a series of missteps, with which I won't bore you, they squandered their leadership position and lost most of their good people and their market. They're now irrelevant to the industry and, like many other people in similar predicaments, extremely touchy about it. I expect brickbats from them for even this simple note. But real geeks, among whom I number myself, miss the old Borland.

at a Tech Ed. There are tables piled high with snacks, usually of the salty/sugary/greasy variety. In California, trays of carrot and celery sticks lay untouched as attendees (yes, and speakers, too) ransacked the Twinkies and Ding Dongs on either side. One speaker warned the attendees, "Hey, go easy on the junk food. It's a long conference, and this is only Tuesday." He was right; the sugar crash hit me around Wednesday afternoon. Computer geeks are mostly young, as the profession hasn't been around anywhere near as long as, say, carpentry. As my college class reunion gifts evolved as we got older, from beer mugs to shot glasses to brandy snifters to 12-step recovery program coffee mugs, I'll bet the Tech Ed cuisine changes as its audience ages. When they take away the Haagen-Dazs bars, I'm not coming back.

WHO SPEAKS, AND WHEN, AND ABOUT WHAT

The main attraction of Tech Ed, of course, is the presentations — 500 or more talks over the course of a week, on every conceivable topic dealing with software development in the Microsoft world. How to do this. How to avoid that. Case studies of what happened when real people tried to do this while avoiding that. The latest enhancements to every conceivable Microsoft product. New styles of software architecture dictated by these emerging changes. Panel discussions featuring industry pundits such as myself. Xbox video gaming tournaments with the action projected on wall-size screens.

The biggest draw recently seems to be the security talks, as that's what's on everyone's mind these days. Steve Riley, always one of the top-rated speakers, presented a talk on social engineering as an attack mechanism. As I discuss in Chapter 3, social engineering is using human interaction to compromise security systems — for example, stealing a password by calling the help desk and asking for it instead of cracking it mathematically. Steve is an engaging speaker, always near the top of the evaluations. His session left no doubt in users' minds that a large problem did indeed exist, but I wish he had said more about the trade-offs involved in solving it. How do you figure out a security policy that keeps you reasonably safe but isn't so obtrusive that you can't live with it?

Of course, if you try that, sometimes it backfires and goes over attendees' heads. I remember an excellent presentation by Erik Olson, the main security architect for Microsoft's Web server system. He explained in detail just what you had to do to secure your user IDs and passwords on your server, what the levels of trade-offs were when you would pick one level versus another, and what vulnerabilities it still left you with. I sat next to several developers from a particular county sheriff's office, watching them shake their heads wondering how the heck they were going to get all that done without screwing it up and what other problems existed that Erik couldn't fit into a one-hour talk.

Tech Ed always has several keynote talks featuring an industry heavyweight like Bill Gates or Steve Ballmer. They get big attendance, but I've mostly stopped going to them. They're too general; they don't provide enough specific knowledge. For example, in San Diego in 2004, Steve Ballmer said that Microsoft had seen the error of its ways and henceforth wouldn't add any new features to its programs until it had made them secure. That's a wonderful sentiment, but until I see specifics of exactly how Microsoft is securing the pieces that I deal with, those lovely sentiments don't help.

Tech Ed is produced by Microsoft, so it's not surprising that what you get there is the story of the world according to Microsoft. When you work primarily in a Microsoft-oriented world—as so many of us do—that's a vital thing to get. But it's necessary to remember that there's another side of the coin you're not getting at Tech Ed. You have to go to other conferences—say, Java One—to hear panel discussions with titles like "Microsoft: Threat or Menace?"

Speakers live or die by their evaluations. The attendees enter them online using the e-mail computers shown previously in Figure 6–1. The results get tallied instantly, and are displayed on monitors throughout the conference. Attendees rate speakers on a numeric scale, and also give specific comments. "Too much of this. Not enough of that. We want more examples. The weasel joke was hysterical. The weasel joke sucked. Your fly was down the whole time. Get a Macintosh."

Speakers constantly monitor their evaluations and compare them to the other speakers'. The best I've ever done was tied for fourth among all speakers that week. The site lists the top ten evaluations, and, more controversially, it also shows the bottom ten. The bottom guy in San Diego was someone I'd met briefly but never worked with. His score was a little over three on a scale of nine, bad news any way you look at it. I didn't go to his talk, but the attendee comments were things like, "He showed up a half-hour late, clearly hung over." (This is a major sin in the eyes of other speakers, to whom performing well with a hangover, especially a visible one, is a highly respected talent.) "His demonstrations didn't work." I don't know if he'll be invited back again.

What I like best about Tech Ed is the chance to see my fellow speakers, the leaders of this industry, the *digerati*. I work mostly by myself or with clients well below my level of expertise. (I don't mean any disrespect by that; I mean, if they weren't, then why would they pay me?) Not that I can't learn from them; I do, all the time. But immersing myself in the sea of sheer brainpower of all those speakers is what I like best about the whole week. Musicians must feel like this when they get to jam with other really good musicians at a music festival.

We talk about what we're doing and what we're trying to do and what we're still banging our heads against, reminisce about this or that previous conference. "Hey, didn't we knock 'em dead in Barcelona last summer? What's your next book topic? How's that publisher treating you?" I can meet in the flesh people whom

I've known only through their work, and others can do the same to me. I love it when someone quotes something from one of my books: "Hey, Dave, your Second Law of the Universe is great: 'The amount of crap in the universe is conserved. If you have less crap over here, you must have more crap over there, because there's no such thing as making it disappear.' It sure describes my project."

The European Tech Ed includes a speaker's party after shutdown on the last night, for which the organizers rented out the old Heineken brewery in Amsterdam. The talks are over, the attendees have gone home, and we don't need to keep our game faces on anymore. We can just relax and enjoy each other's company, because we seldom get a chance to be among that many good brains. Another speaker, a guy I like and who likes my books, said to me: "Plattski, this is fabulous." Gesturing with his pint glass (he'd gotten an earlier start than I had), he continued: "Look at all the great brains here. There's [this smart guy], and there's [that really smart guy], and there's [another really, really smart guy]. And I've earned myself a place at the table with them, and so have you. It's such a blast." I couldn't agree with him more.

I don't suppose that Tech Ed speakers get any more unglued than any other conventioneers, no more than insurance agents or funeral directors or colostomy supply salesmen, and certainly we don't approach the level of Shriners. But seeing all these deep, rational guys letting it all hang out is a blast, albeit not without its dangers. If that video of me singing karaoke, or more accurately *trying* to sing karaoke ("In the jungle, the mighty jungle, the lion sleeps tonight"), ever makes it onto the Internet, I am screwed forever.[2]

---

2. Traveling back from Tech Ed the next day, I couldn't help whistling that tune as I changed planes in London. Someone I couldn't see yelled from the other side of the terminal, "Plattski, will you shut the hell up, already?" Don't worry; I haven't quit my day job yet.

It's exciting seeing new speakers enter the fraternity. One lady, after giving her first-ever talk on Friday afternoon, was still bouncing off the walls from the rush of it at 3:00 a.m., as we were getting thrown out of a bar in Barcelona so that they could close. "Wow, you guys, that was great, is it always like that?" "Alexis," I told her, "you've been bitten by the werewolf. You're one of us now, damned forever to wander the airways of the world, sustained only by that elusive first-class upgrade, eternally seeking that 'speaker's high' that you only get in front of an audience. Welcome, and may God have mercy on you. And you can buy the next round. I think that place down the street is still open."

Of course, anything so powerful is always double-edged. I remember a conference, not a Tech Ed but similar, when a talk I had planned to see got cancelled. "Why was that?" I asked the organizer. "It would have been the second-ever talk of the lady giving it, and she got hammered so badly on the evals of her first talk today that she wouldn't go on again." She'd gotten ripped to shreds by almost everyone, including vicious personal insults from a whole group of attendees, to which the rookie speaker hadn't yet grown a protective skin. And this took place in Canada, where people are reputed to be (and I've always found them to be) nice, so she must have really stunk. Perhaps it's just as well that I missed that talk. As rock climbers find their sport thrilling because only their own skill keeps them from falling, so we speakers thrill to a successful talk, because we've seen other speakers crash in flames, done it ourselves a few times, and know what can happen if we're not good enough, or don't prepare enough, or don't treat the audience with the respect due a barrel of live rattlesnakes.

In some ways, we speakers are competitors, but we have more in common with each other. One of them actually introduced me to the publisher of this book. Not many other people make their living the way we do, and I think we bring out the best in each other when we meet. We rub elbows for a few days; then disperse into the airways again, knowing we'll meet sometime in Redmond or Amsterdam or Singapore.

SELLING IT

In addition to all the talks, Tech Ed also hosts a large tradeshow. Attendees come to Tech Ed to keep up with the latest developments in the industry. While the educational sessions tell them how to write software, the tradeshow displays the products and services that actually do exist today, such as tools they can use in their work.

The exhibit hall is at least the size of a football field, and finding space for it is probably the largest factor dictating the choice of a site. Exhibiting is expensive, starting at $7,000 for the smallest booth, but no vendor to this market can afford to miss 10,000 geeks all in one place. You'll see everything here: software; hardware; palmtop computers and programmable cell phones; books and magazines; training classes, both online and in person. If it has bits, it's here.

As Eric Sink, founder of a company that makes programmer tools, wrote in an online article about the Tech Ed tradeshow, "[It] offers face time. Coming to the show this week will give us the opportunity to meet in person with prospective customers. They will tell us their opinion of our product. They'll ask for features we don't have. We'll have the increasingly rare opportunity to experience the people in our market segment as real people. We also get face time with our competitors and partners ... [and] with some of our existing customers. Throughout this week, people who already use our products will be stopping by the booth to chat. Some will simply want to meet us in person. Some will tell us how happy they are with the product. Some will tell us how we have disappointed them in some way." As you can see, the exhibitors have a busy week.

Vendors come up with all kinds of ways to entice passersby to stop in to their booths. Think of the geeks you know. They're all crazy, of course, but more specifically you know they love toys and fun to a fault. So above all, a vendor's display can't be boring. A Formula-1 race car stopped traffic to advertise the remote sensing software that captured data during a race. The booth of a graphics company

sported a ten-foot Etch-a-Sketch, which people would line up to doo-
dle on. Magicians are a big draw. No geek can resist the analytical
challenge of figuring out how the tricks are done, especially close up.
A free espresso cart is always popular, given geeks' addiction to caffeine. You'd think that pretty girls would be popular with the overwhelmingly male audience, but that doesn't happen very often. I
doubt that's because of political correctness, but rather because geeks
get into their bit-head zone at the start of the conference and don't
come out until the end.[3] One reader reports that a large vendor once
presented the Dallas Cowboy Cheerleaders, but he couldn't remember what the product was or even the vendor's name.

Vendors also compete by giving out free stuff, mostly cheap
junk, in return for contact information. None of the attendees is
poor, making at least $50,000 per year and often twice that or more.
For some strange reason they find this swag, these *tschotchkes*, so irre-
sistible that every attendee is issued a large knapsack at registration
for the purpose of carrying it all. Key rings. Flashlights. Baseball caps.
Yo-yos. Pens that light up. Rubber balls to squeeze in meetings and
imagine it's your manager's throat. Swiss army knives used to be popular (typical geek, no?), but they're out of fashion now that they can't
go through airport security. The company with the big Etch-a-
Sketch gave out miniature ones as premiums. T-shirts are always popular; since they're accepted work attire at most companies, you can
avoid clothes shopping for the whole year if you squirrel away
enough of them.[4] One company said "the heck with this trinket nonsense" and cut straight to the chase, giving out genuine two-dollar

---

3. This attitude is best illustrated by the old geek joke about a programmer who
decides to get a mistress to boost his productivity. When asked how that will help
him churn out code, he says, "Simple. I'll tell my mistress I'm with my wife, I'll tell
my wife I'm with my mistress, and then I can *really* get some work done in the lab!"

4. I once scoured the entire show floor looking for promotional socks because I'd run
out of clean ones, but couldn't find any. There's a promo idea for you; who doesn't
like a nice comfy pair of socks?

bills to anyone who would sit through their sales pitch. I didn't actually see that one, but I'm told the line stretched the length of the show floor.

Once you've decided to stop at a booth, you have to find the right person to talk to. There's always a marketingbozo[5] out front spouting buzzwords that he doesn't understand, hoping to land a customer who would rather buy a product than admit he doesn't understand them either. I remember one waxing poetic about a piece of software, the new revision of which had just been made "object oriented." I won't bore you by defining this buzzword, but it describes the internal structure of the program itself rather than anything a user would care about or even notice. I was getting a little tired of marketingbozos by then, so I shut him up by asking, "Please forgive my ignorance, but exactly what is object-oriented software, how does it differ from non-object-oriented software, and why is that difference something I care about buying?" Watching the marketingbozo wriggle like an insect with a pin through it until the technical guy recognized me and bailed him out and we both laughed at him was the high point of the show for me that year. Call me easily amused.

More than any other quality, a good exhibit is interactive. The attendees have to be able to play with the merchandise. It was one thing to read a description of a three-dimensional interactive graphics helmet. It was a completely different experience to put it on and look around, watching the 3D shapes move as it tracked my head location. Suitably impressed, I then chatted with the vendor on the new techniques that programmers will have to learn to write applications for it, and gave him some suggestions on how that could be made easier. They're still a bit on the expensive side at $5,000 a pop, but simple mass production will bring it down to $1,000 in a couple

---

5. That's a single word I've coined for this express purpose. Not quite as expressive as *idoit*, perhaps, but still useful. It describes the kind of clueless dumbbell that would pour a fortune into an advertising campaign for caffeine-free diet Jolt Cola and wonder why it didn't sell.

years (if the company lasts that long), and then it becomes a high-end Christmas gift. The vendor demonstrated it with a movie meant to show off geometrical shapes, clearly aimed at the gaming market. But when I asked attendees who had tried it what type of content they'd most want to see in it, the unanimous answer was a single one-syllable word: porn. When I asked the vendor how they planned on exploiting that market, they said they had no plans to do so. "If Long Dong Silver hands you a check, you'll tell him to keep his money?" "Yes." I bet his venture capitalist backers would have given a different answer. I didn't want to call him a liar, but he's either that or a fool who won't have his job long.

Vendors give a key ring or a plastic Slinky (isn't that an oxymoron?) to everyone that stops by the booth, but they reserve special treatment for their select friends. The parties at Tech Ed are legendary, and it's a status symbol to get the most invitations even if you don't go to all of them. Private dinners at exclusive restaurants. Booze cruises. Outdoor barbecues with a mechanical bull. Some wingding at the San Diego Zoo that I couldn't wangle a pass for, but that I'm told was great. One Microsoft presenter, whose job entails going to tradeshows about once a month, says, "You really have to bring your stunt liver to these things."

THE NEXT GENERATION OF GEEKS — PASSING IT ON

The most interesting, and possibly the most disturbing, thing that I've ever done at a Tech Ed was to help judge the Imagine Cup programming contest in Barcelona in the summer of 2003. Microsoft sponsors this contest for teams of computer science students. It's entirely up to the students to choose a problem, and then design and implement a software solution to it using the latest Microsoft technology. Besides having fun and hopefully learning something, the 16 finalists get a free trip to Tech Ed and the top three teams share $40,000 of prize money. All teams retain ownership of their inventions.

Eight of us judges, three from the U.S. and the rest from universities around the world, had the job of ranking the contestants. Sixteen teams had advanced to this round; two from the U.S., the balance from Europe, Asia, and South America. All displayed good programming techniques and had surmounted their technical hurdles with ingenuity and imagination. But to this day I still cringe at their lack of problem definition skills, the way they chose which problems they'd surmount. Almost everyone worshiped technology for its own sake, my bugaboo as you've probably learned by now, and yours too. I think a faculty adviser who allows that is letting his students down severely. I shudder to think of these guys getting unleashed on the world in their current state.

For example, the German team (dressed in blazers and ties, the only team so attired) had tried to solve the problem of unchecked password proliferation—requiring different user IDs and passwords for all your many Web accounts, as I wrote about in Chapter 4. Fine, that's a real and nasty problem, but their attempt at solving it demonstrated that they didn't understand why it's so nasty. Instead of typing in a password to gain access to a merchant's Web site, you'd call the team's authentication server from your cell phone, and the caller ID system would authenticate your identity to the merchant Web site. It's the single sign-on idea that I described in Chapter 4, using a piece of hardware that they hoped the customer already has in his pocket.

They didn't think from the standpoint of their customers, neither the users nor the merchant Web sites. To buy a book from Amazon.com, which would you rather do? Type in a password as you do today, or remember where you last left the &%^$*!@ phone, go get it, charge the battery (finding the charger if necessary), turn it on, wait for it to boot up, dial a ten-digit number, then enter another 12-digit order number? When I asked them why a user would buy from a site that made them go to all that trouble, they said, "Because it's safer." They don't realize that ease of use is the main problem in any security system. If users find it too difficult to unlock a secure door, they'll prop it open and disable the alarm sensor, or they'll find a different pathway that isn't locked, or they won't go through it at all. The team also never thought about the chicken-and-egg problem inherent in their design: Which sites would pay for their authentication service until a critical mass of customers register for it, but which customers will register for it until some useful sites accept it? This was a classic example of inventing something without stopping to ask why it would be a useful thing to have. It's about what I'd expect from a country whose language gave us the crossover word *schadenfreude*.[6]

The team from Taiwan had developed a system that identified musical tunes, or tried to. Did you ever wake up in the morning with a tune running through your head that you just can't identify? Me neither. But this team wrote a program that allowed you to dial a phone number and hum the tune into the computer on the other end. The program would figure out which song it was, play it for you, and offer to download it as a ring tone for your cell phone if you punched in your credit card number. It worked OK for the pretty girl team member with the nice voice, but somehow not for me. Maybe my jet-lagged croaking scrambled its circuits, or maybe its database didn't include "Three Day Drunk Looking for a Place to Happen." (Fish Head Music, 1999, www.jim-morris.com. Hey, obscure tunes are, by definition, the ones you're least likely to be able to remember. I'll bet they don't have his 2005 smash hit, "Booze Is the Duct Tape of Life," either.) Again, I found the technology somewhat interesting for its own sake, especially the signal processing mechanisms (OK, I'm a geek). But I'd be lying if I said that fear of waking up with an unidentifiable tune in my head keeps me awake on many nights.

---

6. Pronounced "SHOD-en-froy-duh," it means "delight at someone else's misfortune." When I heard that O.J. Simpson lost his civil suit and had to pay all his money to the Goldmans, I danced a little jig of *schadenfreude*. It's almost as handy as *idoit* and *marketingbozo*, even if I didn't coin it.

Worst of all, to my mind, was the team from Singapore. They said that waiting in a checkout line at a Singapore supermarket can take 20 minutes or more. How that can be true in hyper-efficient Singapore I don't know, but I freely concede they ought to know that sort of thing much better than I do, and I agree that eliminating a 20-minute grocery checkout line would be a great boon to humanity. They'd worked incredibly hard, probably the hardest of any of the teams. They'd written some excellent technical software, and even partnered with the electronic engineering department to develop some new hardware they needed to run it. And they'd come up with the sort of horrible monster that desperately needs drowning at birth.

They'd taken the idea of self-checkout, which I detest and refuse to use when I encounter it at Home Depot or my local supermarket, and put it on wheels, where I detest it even more. They mounted a portable laser scanner onto a shopping cart. When you picked a product off the supermarket shelf, you'd scan it before tossing it into your cart. To keep you honest, the cart would have a weight sensor under the basket, and the weight would have to tally with the items you had scanned. To check out, you'd slide your credit card through a reader on the cart. You'd redeem coupons by placing your infrared-equipped palmtop or cell phone against a smart kiosk display, then holding it under the scanner.

May the gods protect you and me from this awful use of technology for its own sake. In addition to making us do work that someone else now does for us, every user would have to learn and deal with the peccadilloes of a complex technical implementation (see Chapter 1). For example, you couldn't put your purse or coat or packages from other stores in the cart because that'd throw off the weight sensor. If you'd changed your mind after scanning something into the cart, you'd have to scan it again before putting it back on the shelf, and make sure to press the credit button. Toddlers would no doubt be fascinated by the laser scanner ("Lookit! *Ouch!* My eye!"), and so would school-age children ("Cool! A real ray gun! Lemme zap that old lady over there. *Pow!*"), not to mention teenagers (I'll leave that to your imagination). You'd have to read directions, no doubt written in a language that occasionally resembled English, just to buy a candy bar. And of course, each store would use a different type of cart, so you'd have to learn them all. I can think of no way to do greater damage to the world retailing industry, short of an all-out, first- and second-strike nuclear exchange.

A grocery delivery service such as Peapod (www.peapod.com), where you order groceries online and they get delivered to your door, would be a far better solution to this problem. It saves not only the checkout time, but also the shopping time and the transportation time, probably an hour or more each week, and reduces road traffic and energy usage overall. It works profitably in rural Massachusetts where I live, so it ought to make even more money in densely populated Singapore. If you wanted to preserve the in-store shopping cart experience, then radio-frequency ID tags on each package would allow you to tally up a whole cartful simultaneously by pushing one button at checkout instead of individually scanning each item.[7] But the cart-based laser scanner for individual items is a giant step backward.

I placed the Singapore team in the middle of the pack because they had worked harder than anyone else. The other judges, less jaded than I am, or perhaps dedicated more to programming than to usability, placed them higher and they actually tied for third place and won some money. If I'd known they were that close to a prize,

---

7. These actually do exist today, and are in fact starting to be required by such heavy purchasers as the U.S. Department of Defense and Wal-Mart. Currently costing about 25 cents each, they are still too expensive for most individual product packages. They're currently used on individual high-cost items such as TVs, and pallets of low-cost items. But cut the price in half four times, to about a penny apiece, and we'll see them on everything. That's expected around 2010. For more information, see www.autoidlabs.org. On November 15, 2004, the FDA and major pharmaceutical companies announced they would soon be used on pharmacist-size bottles of frequently counterfeited drugs such as Viagra.

I'd have whacked them harder to keep them out. In case you're wondering, I told them all of this when the contest was over.

Fortunately the contest contained one absolute gem. Tu Nguyen's bilingual data entry system for waiters in his family's Vietnamese restaurant blew me away and was the judges' overwhelming choice for the $25,000 first prize. The chef, his father, spoke little English, and bilingual Vietnamese waiters are hard to find in Omaha, Nebraska. If Tu was ever going to escape the role of go-between, he had to find some way to make the restaurant work without him. So he put the restaurant's menu onto a Pocket PC, essentially a paperback-book-size computer with a wireless network They're cheap enough ($200 and falling) so that each waiter could carry one. Waiters would enter the customers' orders in English and send them over the wireless network to an ordinary PC running Tu's server program. This contained a translation table that converted them into Vietnamese and printed them in the kitchen.

In addition to changing languages without human translation, orders got to the chef more quickly because waiters didn't have to walk to the kitchen or queue for a single entry terminal. The wastage rate and flow disruption due to misunderstood orders plummeted, and the angry customer saying "This isn't what I ordered, you [racial epithet]" became a thing of the past. Faster order processing led to faster table turnover in the small restaurant, increasing their sales per square foot. It became possible to reliably tailor a dish to the diner's taste, adding extra broccoli or omitting the cilantro, which increased customer satisfaction, and hence return visits and word-of-mouth publicity. It also improved their reviews in the local media, as professional reviewers always ask for special orders as part of their investigative process.

Instead of using technology for its own sake, Tu focused with laser precision on the business problem he was trying to solve. This small, simple, beautifully tailored system dramatically lowered the friction of almost every aspect of running this restaurant. Replacing the translation table would allow it to work from any language to any other language—say, entering orders in Spanish and having them come out in Japanese. It's under consideration for use in Omaha's new sports stadium, and I imagine that Tu will have his choice of job offers on graduation, if he doesn't run with it himself. Chalk up another immigrant success story for the Land Of Opportunity.

I tried very hard to explain to all the teams that had misunderstood. Computing isn't a technology field anymore, it's a people field. Of all the things that I did at Tech Ed, I think, I *hope* that my influence on these impressionable students, rewarding careful problem definition and punishing technology for its own sake, might just be the biggest contribution I could ever make to the industry—apart, of course, from the book you are now reading.

7
. . .

WHO ARE THESE CRAZY BASTARDS ANYWAY?

Geek (n): Somebody who enjoys and takes pride in using computers or other technology, often to what others consider an excessive degree.
—from a T-shirt hanging in the Microsoft Company Store

The preceding chapter showed you how geeks behave in large groups. Now it's time to look at them individually. It should be clear by now that the main reason software sucks today is that the people who develop it don't understand their user population—its needs and wants, its hopes and fears. Because of that ignorance, and their ignorance of that ignorance, they unconsciously assume that their users are similar to themselves. "I like this," they think to themselves, "and it's obvious to me. Therefore, everyone will like it and everyone will find it obvious. That's only common sense,[1] right?"

HOMO LOGICUS

Wrong. The world view of the geeks who create software is vastly different from the world view held by their users. That shouldn't surprise you. Think how differently doctors see the world compared to their patients—that's not a delicious, lip-smacking, sugar-dripping Krispy Kreme donut, washed down with an eye-opening Starbucks coffee (if their Web site will deign to tell you where the nearest one is; see Chapter 2), it's a heart attack waiting to happen. Think how differently a Catholic archbishop views the world compared to his parishioners—"Hey, what's a few molested altar boys compared to a scandal? Move that priest to a different parish, maybe nobody will notice." As members of these and other professions (think lawyers) often seem to inhabit another world, so do computer geeks. And as people become doctors or priests because that profession's world view appeals to their personalities, so do people become professional programmers because programmers' way of viewing the world and themselves appeals to the geek in them.

Alan Cooper, for whom you might have noticed by now I've expressed an admiration, has coined the term *homo logicus* to designate the programmer subset of people. Let me show you some of the

---

1. This term is the world's greatest oxymoron. Nothing on God's good Earth is less common than sense. The next time you catch yourself saying "common sense" (or "intuitive," which means the same thing), stop and listen to yourself for a second. You probably sound like an idiot, insisting that other people think like you do when you're arguing with them because they clearly don't. Replace that term with "I think," which is what it really means. Then you'll realize that you need to find out what the other person actually does think, instead of what you mistakenly think they think, or wish they thought. That would be an uncommonly sensible thing to do.

ways in which they differ from the rest of humanity. Come on, they won't bite you. Not in these pages, anyway.

TESTOSTERONE POISONING

The first thing you notice at Tech Ed or any other computer conference is that the long lines during the breaks snake out from the men's room rather than the ladies' room. Computer geeks are overwhelmingly male. Exact numbers are hard to come by, but my current advanced programming class is 9 percent female, and last year's was 12 percent. Other faculty members report similar numbers, so I doubt that it's me.[2]

Even within the computing industry, the more hard-core a particular field is perceived as being, the greater is the percentage of its practitioners who are male. In the decade or more that I've been working with Microsoft's low-level plumbing, I can remember only one or two women working in that area of development. Evangelism, management, sales, support, yes; but almost every guy I know who spends all day, every day, up to his elbows in computer entrails is exactly that: a male-gendered guy of the X-Y chromosome persuasion. (Spare me the outraged e-mails from hard-core female programmers. I know you exist and I don't doubt that you're good; there just aren't very many of you. And although you might wish there were more, my wife cautions that you really don't want to wait in the ladies' room lines at the nurses' conference.)

I can't imagine it's a brainpower problem. The smartest student I ever had in 12 years of teaching, the only one who maintained an average of more than 100 percent, was Daphne, a female MIT

---

2. I once publicly reprimanded a female student who asked for a homework extension that she knew was unwarranted. She went to Rosemary, my head teaching assistant, for comfort, saying, "Gosh, Dave isn't real nice to women, is he?" And Rosemary sprang to my defense, saying, "Gender has nothing to do with it. Dave treats *everybody* like scum." Gotta love her.

chemistry graduate. In addition to acing every assignment (and getting them all in on time, which no one else has ever done before or since), she did all of my suggested extra credit projects, plus a few that she thought up on her own just for the sheer pain of it, while also being a full-time mother of two school-age children. Unfortunately for the computing industry, she decided she'd rather create beadwork jewelry (www.daphnesdesigns.com) than write code with a bunch of geeks.

When I asked Daphne why she thought there were so few female programmers, she said: "People often choose their first fields of study in high school, where it's common for kids to hide what they are good at in order to fit in better. And being a geek is ten times worse socially for a girl than a boy. My daughter, a physics geek, has a lot of trouble socializing with the girls, but much less with boys. They tend to forgive social gaffes like talking about quantum mechanics, but the girls have little patience for it. On the other side, my daughter has little patience for talking about hair, clothes, and boys, which is what most of the girls want to talk about."

The practice of medicine has changed greatly in the last 50 years, as the proportion of female doctors went from almost nothing to more than half of today's medical school graduates. Many people think that the recent child molestation and cover-up scandals in the Catholic church stem at least in part from the hierarchy's all-male culture. I can't believe that the heavily male composition of the computer industry doesn't affect the development of software in significant ways. That may be one of the reasons we see stupid, counterproductive, so-called "cool" features like the floating menu bar I wrote about in the introduction, instead of useful things that would help us get real work done. If a significant percentage of programmers were mothers with children, we'd probably see a ruthless prioritization that could only benefit the industry, and society as a whole.

As Paco Underhill wrote in *Why We Buy: The Science of Shopping* (Simon and Schuster, 1999), of his careful study of gender differences in shopping: "Men are in love with the technology itself, with the gee-whiz factor, with the horsepower .... [They're] gathered around the barbecue comparing the size of their hard drives and the speed of their modems. As they say, it's a dude thing." Women, on the other hand, "take a completely different approach to the world of high-tech. They take technologies and turn them into appliances. They strip even the fanciest gizmo of all that is mysterious and jargony in order to determine its usefulness. Women look at technology and see its purpose, its reason—what it can do [for them]. The promise of technology is always that it will make our lives easier and more efficient. Women are the ones who demand that it fulfill its promise." I'd like to see that promise fulfilled, which is one reason I wrote this book. Maybe my daughters will be the ones to make it happen.

CONTROL AND CONTENTMENT

Geeks need to feel that they're in control of their situations at all times. This need probably dates back to grade school. They weren't good in sports, the girls wouldn't talk to them, but they could turn that putty-colored box in the corner on or off anytime they wanted to. And if they told it exactly, *exactly*, down to the last bit, what they wanted it to do, it'd follow those instructions. As I wrote in Chapter 1, geeks like driving stick-shift cars because of the feeling of control that it gives them. They don't mind doing the extra work, both initially to learn how to do it and then constantly shifting gears all day, every day, while they drive. They think that's a good trade-off—that it's how cars ought to work—and they're proud that they're smart enough to recognize it and then do it. They know in the abstract that some people don't agree with them, and regard it as an amusing quirk in what they think is a tiny fraction of the populace. But they can't understand why anyone would feel that way, and are surprised when that tiny minority turns out to be almost everyone.

Because they crave control, geeks constantly analyze how things work and try to figure out ways to make them work better. To make this point in a class, I often ask the students, "When was the last time you felt contentment? Joy, sadness, hunger, anger, especially at me, yes; but I want to know about contentment. When was the last time you felt it? Can you remember having *ever* felt it? This isn't a rhetorical question. I want a date, a time, and a place." No one has yet given me one. Not once. Part of this is societal. Regardless of our wealth, we don't live in a contented age. As Brookings Institution fellow and NFL commentator, Gregg Easterbrook, wrote in *The Progress Paradox: How Life Gets Better While People Feel Worse* (Random House, 2003): "Someday if Eden is ever restored, people may complain about the predictable menu of milk and honey, and about the friendly lions purring too loudly." But even within modern society, programming is an inherently non-contented profession, and it draws practitioners who are temperamentally noncontented people. Of course, to a true geek, the glass is neither half-full nor half-empty. It's twice as big as it currently needs to be, though a reasonable reserve margin is not a bad thing to have ready, just in case.

Programmers spend their days trying to make their software a little better (according to what *they* consider better, which is often not what their users think), and a little better the next day, and a little better the day after that because that's the kind of people they are. It's hard-wired into their psyches; they can't turn it off when they leave the lab. They can't even eat breakfast without wondering to themselves whether there isn't perhaps a better way to do it that a person as smart as they ought to be able to see. Here's an example from *Cryptonomicon* (Arrow, 2000), Neal Stephenson's geek novel:[3]

---

3. Despite *Cryptonomicon*'s length (900+ pages), geeky characters, and plot involving cryptography and advanced number theory, it reached #12 on the *New York Times* bestseller list, and I recommend it highly. If you like *Why Software Sucks*, I think you will probably like *Cryptonomicon*.

"World-class cereal-eating is a dance of fine compromises. The giant heaping bowl of cereal, awash in milk, is the mark of the novice. Ideally one wants the bone-dry cereal nuggets and cryogenic milk to enter the mouth with minimal contact and for the entire reaction between them to take place in the mouth. Randy [the main geek character] has worked out a set of mental blueprints for a special cereal-eating spoon that will have a tube running down the handle and a little pump for the milk, so that you can spoon dry cereal up out of a bowl, hit a button with your thumb, and squirt milk into the bowl of the spoon even as you are introducing it into your mouth. The next best thing is to work in small increments, putting only a small amount of Cap'n Crunch in your bowl at a time and eating it all up before it becomes a pit of loathsome slime, which, in the case of Cap'n Crunch, takes about thirty seconds."

MAKING MODELS

As Frederick Brooks wrote in his classic book *The Mythical Man-Month*, programmers work with "nearly pure thought-stuff." Unlike producers of, say, coffee beans or hand grenades or books like the one you are holding, a programmer produces nothing concrete enough to drop on her foot. A doctor deals with real physical bones or noses or intestines, but a programmer manipulates only mental constructs made by herself or other programmers.

Geeks therefore view the world through abstract mental models in a way that other professions don't. A stack, for example, is a memory structure inside a program organized such that the last piece of information the programmer puts into it is the first piece to come out. It's similar to a stack of papers on your desk, hence the name. A queue is a memory structure inside a program organized such that the first piece the programmer puts into it is the first to come out, similar to a waiting line, hence the name. A packet-switched queue is a queue in which all items awaiting service form one line, and each server, as it finishes its current task and becomes available for a new one, takes the first item from the front of that one line ("Next person in line to window 4, please"). Bank tellers and airline check-in stations are usually organized in packet-switched queues, whereas supermarkets usually have individual queues for each cash register station. "Don't you realize this queue ought to be packet switched!?" a geek will scream to the supermarket manager when he gets stuck behind a senile old lady fumbling for her check-book to buy a candy bar.

Geeks live in these mental models and love them. For example, I spent three weeks last year on a speaking tour with another guy as geeky as I am. One day in the breakfast restaurant I found that I didn't have a fork, so I swiped one from my colleague's place. He joined me soon after and didn't have a fork because I'd taken it it, so he took one from the adjoining table. Another hotel guest soon sat down there and stole a fork from the next table down. My colleague and I argued for days as to whether the stolen fork was moving clockwise around the room, or a "fork hole" or "antifork" was moving counter-clockwise. What would happen when it reached the wall; would it reflect back-ward or would it oscillate between the last two tables? Would it work the same way at dinner as at breakfast or would it work differently, and why? We got to the point of immediately removing a fork from the adjacent table even when we didn't need to so that we could observe its behavior. The only time a waiter noticed the missing fork and replaced it (at the Ritz-Carlton in Lisbon; they pay attention to stuff like that), we said, "Hey, the fork and antifork just annihilated each other. Damn that guy for spoiling our fun."

You're probably thinking that we'd been on the road far too long, and you're probably right. But we don't see ourselves as crazy or weird, though we often enjoy playing that role to the gallery.[4] We

---

4. An excellent way to do this is, when you turn on your computer, to shout out all console output half a second before it appears. It is especially effective if you do it with your eyes closed and fists clenched.

see ourselves as being interested in the world and how it works, as being smart enough to see the abstract patterns that underlie seemingly dissimilar real-world events, as being able to quickly understand a new thing by using these abstract patterns to relate it to something else that we already understand. We pity the people not smart enough to see things that way. The next time you sit down in a restaurant and find your fork missing, look around the room and see whether I'm there, observing and taking notes, the stolen fork sitting brazenly on my table.

GEEKS AND JOCKS

Homo logicus may seem like a completely foreign species, but Alan Cooper points out in his book, *The Inmates Are Running the Asylum* (SAMS, 1999), that you can understand a surprising amount about them if you compare them to a more familiar species: *homo athleticus*, the common jock. At first glance, they couldn't be more different. Jocks are physically coordinated, geeks aren't. Jocks were the center of attention and respect in high school, geeks were exactly the opposite. The girls flocked around football players, most of whom (not all, Brian) were dumb as rocks. A straight-A average was mucho uncool (mine would have been if I'd had one), and even my chess championship trophy couldn't compete with a varsity letter. Although I knew that in the long run I'd make far more money than the high-school jocks (which, as my father pointed out, is far more attractive to the opposite sex), it still burned. Society has looked askance at us ever since the first cave-geek examined a sharp stone and said, "Cool fractal patterns. I wonder if it would scale to spearhead size." "Go tackle a mammoth with your bare hands like a Neanderthal," the cave-jock would roar. Like the late Rodney Dangerfield, we geeks still yearn for respect and appreciation.

Yet the two groups share many similarities. In my undergraduate days, the guys who knew their way around an operating system were even called "computer jocks." Jocks and geeks are both proud, the former of being athletic and the latter of being smart.[5] Because they're both proud, they're both highly competitive, especially within their peer group, although the geek competition isn't immediately visible to outsiders as it involves brain rather than brawn. And both groups ruthlessly stomp on the less able, particularly outsiders, whom they consider unworthy of consideration. Think of the writers of modern computer viruses—not the ones that try to steal money, those guys you can understand as common crooks. Think of the ones that crash systems just for the pleasure of disrupting them, and compare them to the jock bullies you've known. They're closer than you think.

The jocks had to change their ways after high school, as employment bosses and drill sergeants made them toe the line in ways their teachers never could. Geeks didn't have to change anywhere near as much. On the contrary, since their skills became necessary to society in a way that throwing a ball isn't, they became even nastier. Cooper writes, "It has become perfectly acceptable behavior to administer mental wedgies with inscrutable software, or to snap emotional towels at long-suffering humans just trying to get some cash from their ATM."

That needs to change in the geek world for software to stop sucking. As a parent tells roughhousing, older children: "Hey, be careful of the little ones." Geeks aren't playing only with each other today, like they were 20 years ago. In fact, they're vastly outnumbered today by noncombatants: their users, their customers, the guys who pay their salaries. Software doesn't suck because it has to, as geeks have bamboozled the public into believing. When it sucks, it does so because bad programmers wrote it that way, because they didn't give a damn about their users. We wouldn't accept this behav-

---

5. This leads to another law that I've coined, titled Platt's Programmer Paradox, which states simply that we're smart enough that we could do anything we wanted to, and dumb enough that we choose this line of work. Go figure.

ior from our doctors or airline pilots. Why should we accept it from geeks? We shouldn't. I'll say more about this in my closing chapter.

JARGON

One of the main ways in which any closed group excludes outsiders is through jargon, a private language that only they speak. Priests speak Latin, kindergartners speak Pig Latin, and the thieves in Charles Dickens's *Oliver Twist* had their own cant, in which the Artful Dodger spoke of "japanning his trotter-cases" (cleaning his boots). It shouldn't surprise anyone that geeks also speak their own language that nongeeks can't penetrate. When I get started rattling with a couple of my programmer friends, my wife just shrugs and says, "It's all geek to me." I tried very hard to keep geek-speak out of this book, to avoid scaring you, the buyer and reader. You'd be surprised how difficult I found it.

Besides new words for their abstract mental models, geeks like to coin acronyms, where the initial letters of the words in a phrase are combined to form a new word. The familiar word *radar*, for example, started life as an acronym for radio detection and ranging, and the ubiquitous *modem* came from modulator/demodulator. Doctors are especially famous for using acronyms: "ICU, stat. Dang, he's DOA, GDI" (Intensive Care Unit, Dead On Arrival, God Damn It). The military is another great source. The acronyms SNAFU and FUBAR, which originated there, have become so common that my word processor's spellchecker automatically recognizes them. Geeks use acronyms like DLL (dynamic link library, you see them a lot in Windows) and SDK (software development kit). Being geeks, however, we've gone one step further by coining an acronym for this type of acronym. They're called TLAs, where TLA stands for Three-Letter Acronym. Of course, TLA itself is a TLA.

Being geeks, we quickly realized that the problem with TLAs is that there are only 17,576 unique TLAs in a 26-letter alphabet, and Microsoft used them all up the summer before last. We could get a few more by admitting special characters such Ð and Þ, but these don't appear on many keyboards outside of Iceland.[6] Instead, geeks have increased the length of their acronyms, coining such ones as WSDL (Web Service Descriptor Language) and SOAP (Simple Object Access Protocol).[7] This type of acronym hadn't been named until, in a 1998 newsletter article, I declared them to be FLAPs. This stands for Four-Letter Acronym Package, and of course, FLAP itself is a FLAP.

This gives us 456,976 different combinations, but it took modern geekery less than 20 years to progress enjoying the expansiveness of computers with 64,000 characters of memory to screaming at the inadequacy of computers with 64,000 *times* that amount, or more than 4 billion characters. So I expect the supply of FLAPs to be exhausted quickly. To be prepared, I coined the acronym FLEAP (Five-Letter Extended Acronym Package; FLEAP itself is a FLEAP), which provides almost 12 million different combinations. Geeks used this for OLEDB (I won't bore you with the definition), and our old friends SNAFU and FUBAR are also FLEAPs. And when we run out of FLEAPs, we can use my coinage of SLEAPE, pronounced "sleepy." Inspired by a trip to Canada, it stands for Six-Letter Extended Acronym Package, Eh? There are more than 300 million SLEAPEs in a 26-letter alphabet, which ought to hold us for a little while. Early experiments with SLEAPEs have produced the mellifluous MOOTWA (Military Operations Other Than WAr), which is what they call nation-building in Iraq and hurricane relief

---

6. Still used in modern Icelandic, these characters are holdovers from the Old Norse from which it derives. The former character is named "eth" and has the sound of voiced "th" as in "though." The latter is named "thorn," like the spiky things on roses, and has the sound of unvoiced "th" as in "thought," or thorn itself, or for that matter, the end of eth.

7. As the Holy Roman Empire was neither holy nor Roman nor an empire, so the so-called Simple Object Access Protocol is anything but simple and has nothing whatsoever to do with objects (a popular programming technique). Geeks can't resist a cool acronym, even when it's not completely accurate.

in Louisiana, though I'm not sure if it really should count since the last A doesn't stand for its own word. For geek SLEAPEs, we have PCMCIA, which originally designated a type of expansion card for notebook PCs, but quickly came to stand for the phrase, "People Can't Memorize Computer Industry Acronyms." And of course, SLEAPE itself is a SLEAPE.

BRAINS AND CONSTRAINTS

Geeks especially admire brilliant thought when it is exercised in the face of external constraints. It's like a jock whipping someone with one hand tied behind his back, or a peacock surviving with a huge ornamental tail. "If a guy can crank out that incredible solution within those restrictions," geeks think to themselves, "how much more brilliant must he really be?"

One of their favorite arbitrary constraints is haiku, the Japanese poetry form of three nonrhyming lines, with five, seven, and five syllables. In February of 1998, *Salon* magazine ran a contest in which readers were invited to rewrite a computer error message in haiku.[8] Peter Rothman won honorable mention for:

> Windows NT crashed.
> I am the blue screen of death.
> No one hears your screams.

Charlie Gibbs described most programmers' view of the unfortunate and boring necessity of a program communicating with its users:

> Errors have occurred.
> We won't tell you where or why.
> Lazy programmers.

---

8. Haikus reprinted here originally appeared in the Feb. 10, 1998, edition of the Web magazine *Salon*.

The grand prize went to David Dixon for describing universal events:

> Three things are certain:
> death, taxes, and data loss.
> Guess which has occurred.

Here's one I wrote just after a trip to Toronto:

> My cat pressed Reset.
> Now she's a tennis racket.
> No more furballs, eh?

The platinum-iridium standard for geek haiku is titled "DeCSS Decryption." A team of Europeans reverse-engineered a DVD-player program to crack the encryption scheme that prevented the copying of DVD movies. The resulting decryption program was banned in the U.S. under the Digital Millennium Copyright Act because it was primarily intended to perform illegal actions. However, instructions on how to write such a program are much harder to ban than the program itself because of First Amendment protection of free speech. To give the decryption instructions an artistic value, hence entitling them to even greater First Amendment protection as a work of art, a demented geek (and I mean that in the most complimentary sense of the term, which, because he's a true geek, I know he'll understand) named Seth Schoen rewrote the instructions as a stunning 456-stanza haiku, maintaining the five-seven-five syllable meter throughout. I won't show the whole thing (a link to it appears on this book's Web site), but here's just a taste:

> Now help me, Muse, for
> I wish to tell a piece of
> controversial math,

> for which the lawyers
> of DVD CCA
> don't forbear to sue:

> that they alone should
> know or have the right to teach
> these skills and these rules.

I have shown this haiku to many geeks. Their universal reaction is to shake their heads in admiration, often whispering a reverent "Holy shit." I've seriously thought of hanging up my haiku pen, figuring I'd never accomplish anything remotely close to Schoen's masterpiece. But before so doing, I need to salute him, in haiku, of course:

> Someone with enough
> Time on his hands to write this
> Must have no mortgage.

> I am astounded,
> Awed, amazed, flabbergasted.
> Ye gods, what a geek.

SEVEN HABITS OF GEEKS

Humorist Po Bronson, spoofing Steven Covey's best-selling book *The Seven Habits of Highly Effective People*, coined "The Seven Habits of Highly Engineered People." They are:

1. They will be selfish in their generousness, and they will attempt to look generous in their selfishness.
2. Blindness improves their vision.
3. They'll not only bite the hand that feeds them, but they'll bite their own hand.

4. They will try very hard to maintain the image that they care not at all about their image.
5. They will keep fixing what's not broken until it's broken.
6. I didn't answer incorrectly; you just asked the wrong question.
7. Consider absence of criticism a compliment.

I laughed out loud when I first read them, as no doubt Bronson had intended. But they nagged at me and kept me awake for quite some time until I looked them over more carefully. On further reflection, I decided that Bronson had spoken truth, probably more than he realized. Here's how geeks live up to Bronson's billing.

1. "They will be selfish in their generousness, and they will attempt to look generous in their selfishness." We saw this in Chapter 1, where programmers expose a program's internal workings directly to avoid having to understand who their users are and what they really need, and then design software that makes it easy for them to get it done. The classic example is using confirmation in a program, constantly asking the user, "Are you sure you want to do that? Really sure? Really, really, really sure?" Instead of making actions undoable, which is great for users but hard to program, they wash their hands of responsibility and dump the decision on the user. "Hey, you save when you want to, and throw it away if you don't want to. If you're too stupid to do that, you're an idiot that shouldn't be touching a computer." The programmers call this power. Wrong. It's called bad programming. Lazy programming. Even, to use the most toxic word in the geek vocabulary, stupid programming. And it needs to stop.

2. "Blindness improves their vision." We also saw that in Chapter 1. Remember how a bad program asks "Do you want to save changes?" before writing a file back to the disk? The user interface designer knew too much about how the program was implemented internally, probably because the same person wrote both parts, and she expected the user to learn it as well. If she knew less about how the program was implemented internally, she wouldn't get distracted by its internal implementation. She'd focus solely on the user and his needs. She'd design a better user interface if she could see less of the program, as a blind person gains much more information from hearing the same sounds that a sighted person does.

3. "They'll not only bite the hand that feeds them, but they'll bite their own hand." In Chapter 2, we saw UPS biting the hand that feeds them, the customers who pay them to deliver packages. Their Web site required every single user to manually enter his country before it would talk to him at all, as opposed to Google figuring it out automatically. They don't realize that they're also biting their own hands, but they are. A Web site that is easier to use attracts users. One that's harder to use scares them off. One day UPS will wake up and see that the competition has written a better Web site and stolen their users away. Only that's not stealing customers; that's getting business the old-fashioned way: *earning* it, by figuring out what the customers want (even if they're not sure of it themselves) and then giving it to them.

4. "They will try very hard to maintain the image that they care not at all about their image." I've shown you throughout this book how geek culture values intelligence above any other quality. And what name is synonymous with the absolute highest level of human intelligence? Einstein, of course. His influence (see Figure 7–1) on the dress and (as Stephen Landsburg points out) the grooming habits of generations of geeks is difficult to overstate. Geeks sneer at "Dress for Success" books because in their world, success is measured by the intellectual approval of their peers. The word *suit* is a derogatory term for a manager who doesn't know which end of a soldering iron to hold. It's a *homo logicus* thing, displaying to others, "Hey, we're smart enough that we don't have to play by your rules." It's the visible manifestation of the geek self-image. But the geek code of disdaining dress is every bit as rigid as the one they reject.

FIGURE 7-1 Einstein's trademark disheveled look

I've seen, more than once, a geek care so much about his image of not caring about his image that he turned down a job paying $10,000 more because he would have had to wear a tie to work.

5. **"They will keep fixing what's not broken until it's broken."** Or as Canadian sitcom character Red Green would say: "If it ain't

broke, you're not trying." I discussed this tendency in Chapter 1. Geeks concentrate on making complex things possible instead of on making simple things simple. AT&T directory assistance wasn't broken; it worked just fine when it simply told you the number you had asked for, repeated it so that you could write it down, and hung up. Then the AT&T geeks added the ability to automatically dial the number, for which you pressed a telephone button after the voice had told you the number. It still worked well, so clearly something had to change. The geeks then made it so that the user had to accept or reject auto-dialing before hearing the number, adding seven separate physical motions to every single directory assistance request even if you didn't want auto-dialing. They called this an "improvement." If their goal was to drive down use of directory assistance, they succeeded admirably. AT&T, "Ma Bell," inventor of the transistor and the laser, is now defunct. History. Toast.[9] Coincidence? You tell me.

6. "I didn't answer incorrectly; you just asked the wrong question." What clearer example of this can there be than the Starbucks store locator Web page that I discussed in Chapter 2? I wanted the Starbucks store nearest my ZIP Code, and it said that it couldn't

---

9. The company now known by the name AT&T used to be called SBC, the former Southwestern Bell created by the breakup of the original AT&T in 1983. They bought the decayed remnants of the original AT&T in 2005 for the relative pittance of $16 billion, roughly Microsoft's profits in that year. In what will surely go down as one of the most boneheaded business moves ever, they decided to rename the entire entity AT&T, even spending a fortune to convert their successful Cingular wireless operations to that name after spending millions to rebrand their previously acquired AT&T Wireless as Cingular. They're undoubtedly doing that because their senior management came up through the ranks when the name AT&T in the telecommunications industry meant, quite simply, God. But that name means little to any customer under the age of about 30 and rising, because that company had become irrelevant by the time those customers started paying attention to such things. I say to SBC management, as I've said to so, so many companies in the course of this book, go back and read my first chapter, and engrave my maxim on your heart: Your user is not you.

find one. If there's even one Starbucks store in the entire universe, then there must be one that's nearest my house. It might be around the corner, it might be across the country, it might be on Mars, but one store has to be nearest. The Web site said that it didn't exist. Only after much wrangling did I notice a control that limited the search radius to five miles, and the nearest store turned out to be eight miles away. "You asked me whether there was a store within five miles, and I told you the answer," the Web site says. I didn't ask the wrong question, turkey. You asked it for me.

And Finally

7. **"Consider absence of criticism a compliment."** Geeks not only consider absence of criticism a compliment, but they also consider it to be the highest compliment, in fact, the only compliment worth giving or receiving. Think about it—when was the last time a phone call from work awoke you at 4:30 a.m. on your day off to say, "Everything's running just fine here, no problems at all, hope you have a nice day, we sure are, so go back to bed"? If things are quiet, then they must be going well. The silence that you, dear reader, allow them to bask in, they think is great. When I explain to the UPS.com guys what dunderheads they've been with their language selection process, their defense is to say, "Well, no one's complained up until now."

That's partly because the feedback section of their Web site is as difficult to use as the rest of it, as I discussed in Chapter 2. You have to work your way down through five separate screens with cryptic names to reach the feedback form, then fill out seven separate sections before they'll allow you to submit it. (I'll put a link on this book's Web site to make the process easier, so you can bombard them.) But it's also because you didn't know that things could be and should be better; that your software didn't have to suck and that it shouldn't. Now you do. Read Chapter 9 and I'll tell you how.

8
. . .

MICROSOFT:
CAN'T LIVE WITH 'EM AND
CAN'T LIVE WITHOUT 'EM[1]

Let's face it. Disclaimers to the contrary, Microsoft runs the software world, to the extent that anyone does. If we want software to stop sucking, Microsoft is the main vendor that we need to work on. Even for the portions of the world that they don't run, such as Web servers based on Sun or IBM machines, Microsoft elevating their game will require other vendors to raise theirs, as the availability of good coffee at hundreds of Starbucks stores (see, for example, the Internet humor column reading "New Starbucks to open in men's room of existing Starbucks") has compelled other sellers of coffee to improve theirs.

THEY RUN THE WORLD

No person or even organized group can influence Microsoft an enormous amount; they're too big for that. But if you know how

---

1. Or, as my barber likes to say, "Can't live with 'em, and can't shoot 'em either."

they think, you'll see that there are ways of engaging Microsoft that are more productive and ways which are less. As the companion chapter (Chapter 7) shows you how geeks view themselves, so this chapter attempts to show you how Microsoft views itself. And it will also show you that it's harder being Microsoft than you might think.

You can see Microsoft's relationship to the world in the jokes that people tell about them. I'll toss one out every now and then in this chapter.[2] Like any good parable, they contain a nugget not necessarily of truth, but at least of thought, in a spoonful of sugar that helps the medicine go down. For example, the rapid circulation of the following indicates a widespread belief that Microsoft rules the software world with a heavy hand and sometimes isn't very innovative:

Q: *How many Microsoft programmers does it take to change a light bulb?*
A: *None. Bill Gates just declares Microsoft® Darkness™ to be the new standard.*

ME AND THEM

Before launching into my discussion of Microsoft, I need to fully disclose my relationship with them. I am not now, nor have I ever been, nor am I likely to become after Bill Gates reads this book, a Microsoft employee. I sometimes consult for them on a part-time basis or teach to them or on their behalf, and have done so on and off since 1994. My dollar volume from these ranges from high five figures in a fat year to zero in a lean one. The last two years have been medium, and this year seems to be shaping up the same way.

I own 1,300 shares of Microsoft stock, current value about $31,000, which I bought at full price on the open market in 2000 and 2001. Its value has risen by about 11 percent in five years,

---

2. I don't know who originally wrote any of them, although I will gladly credit in future printings of this book anyone who supplies proof (not just claims) of authorship.

roughly what a passbook savings account would have done over that time. That's worse than some tech stocks (Amazon.com, up 60 percent in that period) and better than others (Sun Microsystems, down 94 percent). I'd be lying if I said that I hadn't hoped for better, but so did many other people. It's worth more money than I started with, so I can't complain too much.

I've written and continue to write books for Microsoft Press and articles for *MSDN Magazine*, their journal for developers. Although neither of these pays much, they provide me with exposure and credibility, in a manner similar to my teaching gig at Harvard Extension, including the low pay. At the same time, not being a Microsoft employee provides me with a different type of credibility. Clients often hire me because they feel that I'm close enough to Microsoft to know what's really going on, but independent enough to give them the straight dope rather than the party line that all large corporations spout. As Microsoft becomes, as they must become and as they are becoming, a larger, stodgier corporation, I expect this consulting line to grow.

Within Microsoft, I have a reputation as a gadfly. Because I'm not a direct employee, I can call things as I see them, can say that the emperor has no clothes, in a way that employees with immediate career paths cannot. Not that anyone listens all that much. Here are several examples that I've written in Microsoft Press books:

"Remember how Windows 1 and 2 flailed around irrelevantly for about five years? Microsoft practically gave them away in Cracker Jack boxes, and still no one would use them because they didn't offer enough useful, convenient, time-saving features.... Windows 3.x [was] a pretty good MS-DOS multitasker that also played Solitaire, and the rest is history." (*Understanding COM+*, 1999, p. 3.)

"I am trying to get the Oxford English Dictionary to accept a word I coined in [an online magazine column]. The word is MINFU, patterned after the military acronyms SNAFU and FUBAR that have crossed into common usage. In polite company,

MINFU stands for <u>MI</u>crosoft <u>N</u>omenclature <u>F</u>oul-<u>Up</u>, and it happens a lot. For example, referring to in-place activation of an embedded object as 'visual editing' (to distinguish it from tactile editing, I guess, or perhaps olfactory editing) is a MINFU.... If I can get it into the Microsoft Press Style Guide, I'll have it made." (*Introducing Microsoft .NET, Third Edition*, 2003, p. 127.)

"The design of [a geeky piece of software] originated in the late 1990s, those euphoric days of the first Web platinum rush, with the NASDAQ index shooting through 3000 en route to 5000. Marketing types, crazed on their own hot air, turned cartwheels, shouting, 'HOORAY! YOUR CELL PHONE WILL GET SPORTS SCORES AND STOCK UPDATES!!!' No one stopped to ask, 'Hey, does anyone really care about that except as a short-lived curiosity for sexually frustrated geeks with nothing better to do on a lonely Saturday night?' And no one asked how anyone was going to make any money with it. Most people had the notion that Web content should somehow be free, a hopelessly naive ideology sneered at today as 'dot-communism.'... The giant cross-platform orgy never happened, despite sensuous lubrication with tons of Microsoft snake oil, and the NASDAQ is currently down around 2000." (*The Microsoft Platform Ahead*, 2004, pp. 67–68.)

Now that you know how Microsoft and I fit together, you can give that relationship whatever weight you think it should have when you read what I say about them, in this chapter and the rest of this book. I'm nicer to them than some of their critics, but you've already seen me come down on them hard for specific technical issues—remember in the introduction when I accused them of "wasting roughly 27 human life spans every single day" with just one bad feature. Doubtless I'll get called an ass-kissing shill by some readers and a vindictive cheap-shot bastard by others, but that's the lot of any writer who calls 'em as he sees 'em on anything, anywhere. Like a chef cooking chili for a large group of people, I'm aiming for roughly equal numbers of complaints that my treatment of Microsoft is too hot or is too mild.

Q: Did you try those new Microsoft-brand condoms yet?
A: Yeah, but first I had to download the patch.

WHERE WE CAME FROM

I remember a plane ride back in 1992, on my way to yet another software conference. Windows 3.1 was brand new then, I was ramping up for my debut teaching it at Harvard Extension, and we were just starting to discuss Windows NT (their first attempt at an industrial-strength operating system, which would ship the following summer). I was wearing a Microsoft T-shirt from a previous conference, which combined the excellent qualities of being a) very comfortable and b) free. "Congratulations, Microsoft," a fellow passenger told me. "Your market capitalization just passed General Motors'." "I don't work for Microsoft," I said, "but I'll let you buy me a beer on their behalf." "Sure thing! They're free here in first class anyway. I'll even buy you two."

That watershed event (the market capitalization, not the free beer) had appeared in the newspapers a few days before. People were flabbergasted, not just that a new economy company had passed an old economy company, but that the new company owned essentially no assets as the term was then understood. Microsoft was profitable, certainly; it wasn't like the Internet bubble companies that we'd see a decade later, with billion-dollar valuations for companies hemorrhaging money with no end in sight.[3] But despite Microsoft's profits, the company produced nothing tangible, nothing you could drop on your foot, in fact, nothing but a magnetic pattern of ones and zeros that an ordinary human couldn't easily distinguish from random noise. But if you

---

3. The classic example of this sort of company is Blue Mountain, which sent customized electronic greeting cards via e-mail. They were bought for $780 million in 1999, and were sold for $35 million two years later.

put a floppy disk containing those ones and zeros into one of those beige boxes you got at the computer store, they would make the dots on its screen dance in this pattern rather than that one, and this control had great value. In fact, the aggregate judgment of Wall Street investors said they valued that control of dancing electrons more than the possession of assembly plants filled with metal-bashing machinery that had within living memory helped win two world wars.

Microsoft was seen then as the good guys in the computer world. Before the advent of the inexpensive personal computer, accomplishing a computing job took a huge effort. The hardware was at least the size of a refrigerator, cost more than a million dollars to buy with high ongoing maintenance costs, and generally required an air-conditioned room, specially controlled electric power, and full-time administrators. The modern spreadsheet, now ubiquitous, didn't, couldn't, exist then. Nor did computer games, nor online porn.

That was a completely different world, one that the half of humanity under about age 35 can't remember. Personal computers and the operating systems that made them go meant computing for the masses. I could write a document without kowtowing to the high priest in the glass house, or play a game without the bluenoses yelling at me for wasting expensive computer time. And if programs crashed now and again, and didn't have a mile-long list of features that I never used anyway, this was still infinitely more than I had just a year or two before. It was like the early Model T Fords opening up transportation to ordinary people, allowing individuals to go where they pleased when they pleased, freeing them from the chains of railroad routes and schedules and fares.

> Programmer #1: *"I hear that if you play the Windows 95 CD backward, you get a satanic message!"*
> Programmer #2: *"That's nothing. If you play it forward, it installs Windows 95!"*

WHY IT SUCKS TODAY

People don't think of Microsoft that way anymore. They're seen as a monopoly, the evil empire. Bill Gates appears (I would suspect unauthorized) on T-shirts (see Figure 8–1) as the all-consuming Borg from *Star Trek: The New Generation* ("Resistance is futile! You will be assimilated!"). We got one of those for a friend of mine when he took a job with Microsoft and moved to Seattle. They've gone from spunky, admired underdog to fearsome 900-pound gorilla in less than a decade. Google's unofficial motto, "Don't be evil," is more a slap at Microsoft than anything else.[4]

It's a public perception problem somewhat similar to Israel's, on a faster time scale. Like Israel, Microsoft is finding out that being

FIGURE 8-1 Bill Gates as the Borg

---

4. As this book went to press, Google had just agreed to censor the Web searches of users in China. Google CEO Eric Schmidt said, "We actually did an Evil-Scale and figured out which is less evil," leading others to quip, "Maybe their motto should 'Do *less* evil.' "

on top isn't quite as much fun as it looked like it would be when it was on the bottom. Not that either of them wants to or can go back to where they were, but neither are their current positions the beds of roses from their earlier imaginations.

That shouldn't surprise you. Think of every piece of growing up you've ever done or seen or even heard of. Remember how, as a kid, you thought how great it would be to be a grownup? You'd stay up as late as you wanted, put your card in an ATM and out would come money, with which you could buy all the candy you wanted and eat nothing else all day long. And then when you did, at least nominally, grow up, you found that you actually did need some amount of sleep, that you first had to earn the money that the ATM dispensed, and that you had to pay for the candy not only at the store but also again at the gym and the dentist. Not that you want to go back, or can, and not that there aren't compensations, like fast cars and sex and good microbrews, but the other side wasn't anywhere near as green as you had previously thought. That's where Microsoft is today.

Microsoft isn't loved today as it was before. This puzzles them, because they can remember when they were the darlings of the media and the world, cheered on by the masses who thought they were improving the world and all of our lives.[5] But that change should, must, always does, happen when someone grows up. My eight-month-old daughter looked unimaginably cute smearing sweet potatoes all over her face in the process of getting just a few into her mouth (see Figure 8–2), and we cheered her on because it represented a new level of accomplishment. She looked a whole lot less cute doing it at age three, attempting to share the cheers we were giving her baby sister for *almost* feeding herself strained carrots. (She'll kill me if I print that picture; I'm in

---

5. Google occupies that position today, although one wonders whether the two founders' purchase of a Boeing 767 wide-body aircraft for their personal use won't change that.

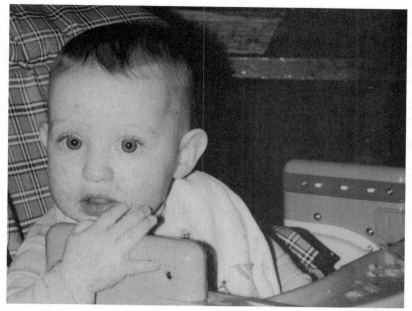

FIGURE 8-2 Sweet Potato Girl. Cute at age 8 months, not so cute at 36 months.

enough trouble for the first one.) We happily tolerated the quirks and bugs of the first word processor spellcheckers because we hadn't had that functionality before. After not too long a time, the quirks moved from cute to irritating and the unfixed bugs got old, and we said, "You're three years old now, big girl. Can't you get those damn sweet potatoes in your mouth? Grow up, already." Microsoft hasn't completely realized this, but they're starting to.

As with anyone who struggles to the top, Microsoft is acutely paranoid about losing their leadership position. They're too big for that to happen, you say? Two words: General. Motors. The former automotive leader is now widely thought to be in a death spiral. Want one more? Digital. As in Digital Equipment Corporation, the old DEC (pronounced like the floor of a ship). Remember them? They used to be the world's second-largest computer company, after

IBM. They misjudged the PC revolution, shrank for a few years, then what was left of them got swallowed by Compaq, a PC maker, in 1998, after which Compaq got swallowed by Hewlett-Packard in 2002. Microsoft worries about this happening to them. Good thing, too. Neither GM nor DEC knows to this day just what hit them (psst, I'll let you in on the secret: products customers didn't like at prices customers wouldn't pay). To Microsoft's credit, this paranoia is forcing them to listen to their customers much more than they used to.

More than anything else in the world, Microsoft desperately wants to shed the "toy" image that they garnered in the early 1990s. Every person has his hot buttons, the little things that someone says or does to him that sends him through the ceiling. I won't ask yours, and I won't tell you mine. But for Microsoft, it's speaking of them as a toy maker. Think of your teenage son's outrage when he gets handed a children's menu at a restaurant, then multiply it by a $40 billion company and you'll understand what I mean. Microsoft thinks of itself as ready to run the mission-critical infrastructure of the world, the back-end processing of banks, not just their desktop word processors. And if that causes them to be proud of how far they've come, regardless of how much farther they might have to go, and sometimes to lack social graces in a way perceived by outsiders as arrogant (again, resembling Israelis), that's just how they are.

Many Internet chain mails are written as spoof business press bulletins, announcing Microsoft's impending acquisition of this or that major institution. The Catholic Church is often mentioned, with the Pope becoming a senior vice president of Microsoft, Steve Ballmer joining the College of Cardinals, and Microsoft bundling a free indulgence with every upgrade to Office. Microsoft is sometimes alleged to be patenting the numbers zero and one, patterns of which comprise all computer programs. "After their successful defense of zero and one, Microsoft lawyers are expected to file liens on infinity and pi this week."[6] *My favorite is the one announcing Microsoft's forthcoming purchase of The People's Republic of China: "Rumors of Bill Gates elevating his title to 'Emperor,' however, are merely speculative at this point."*

DAMNED IF YOU DO, DAMNED IF YOU DON'T

Most of you readers will have some memory of Microsoft facing an antitrust suit from the U.S. Department of Justice. In the fall of 1998, the DOJ and 20 state attorneys general filed *U.S. v. Microsoft*, accusing Microsoft of using monopoly power to drive competitors out of business by, among other things, bundling their Internet Explorer browser into the Windows operating system. In the spring of 2000, Judge Thomas Penfield Jackson ruled that Microsoft had violated antitrust laws and called for Microsoft to be split into two separate companies, known facetiously as "Baby Bills," after the "Baby Bells" that AT&T got divided into.[7]

Microsoft, of course, appealed the verdict. The appeals court panel, while confirming Jackson's findings of fact, unanimously vacated his remedy and removed him from the case for misconduct, primarily speaking improperly to the press during the case. "The final section [of the appeals court ruling], [entitled] 'Judicial Misconduct,'

---

6. You may laugh, but Microsoft really is attempting to patent the single word *IsNot*, when used in a computer language. See U.S. patent application number 20040230959 at www.uspto.gov. The application is pending at the time of this writing, and it is not yet clear whether Microsoft will succeed in patenting the fusion word *IsNot* in a language that already contains the public domain keywords *Is* and *Not* (used separately). Bill Clinton would probably say that it depends on what your definition of *IsNot* isn't.

7. For a detailed description of this particular lawsuit, see the business case written by Nicholas Economides at New York University, currently online at www.stern.nyu.edu/networks/exmba/microsoftcase.pdf. If it moved, Google for his name; it's a good article.

flays him for being an idiot," wrote legal analyst Dahlia Lithwick in Slate.com.[8] A new judge was appointed to consider the remedy, and with a new administration taking charge in Washington, a settlement was reached in 2001. The final settlement terms are highly technical and deal with the internals of the software, so I won't bore you with them, other than to note that they left both plaintiff and defendant wondering what the point had been. Nor will I argue the truth or falsehood of the accusations here, but I want you to keep in mind for the next four paragraphs that the main accusation against Microsoft was using its market power to restrict consumer choice.

At around the same time, Sun Microsystems sued Microsoft over Sun's programming language, named Java. Making a large splash around 1996, Java's main benefit was that it supposedly allowed programmers to write programs that would run on any platform—the exact same program would run on Windows and Macintosh and Linux and any other computer for which Java existed. "Write once, run everywhere," was Sun's slogan for it. As someone who has tried it several times, I can tell you that writing a program that runs properly on multiple platforms was and is much more difficult than Sun claims, particularly when a user interface is involved. It's not just "run everywhere"; I've found it more like "test, debug, and special-case everywhere."[9]

However, as a pure programming language, Java was a big advance over C++ ("see plus plus"), the language of most Windows

---

8. See "Microsoft Bad, Judge Jackson Worse," by Dahlia Lithwick, posted on Slate.com on June 28, 2001.

9. To give just one small example, a Macintosh mouse has only one button, whereas a Windows mouse has two or more. Clicking the right mouse button in a Windows program usually brings up a menu of commands that are available at the site of the click, a "context menu" it's called. A Java program attempting to cover both platforms needs to figure out which one it's running on at any given time and follow the user interface conventions that users of that type of computer expect. Otherwise, the Java program's behavior will be different from that of other applications on the platform, which users will not tolerate.

development at that time. For example, Java automatically recovers pieces of memory that a programmer has finished using, instead of requiring the programmer to spend time and effort cleaning up after himself, as does C++. If you think of an invisible maid following you around the kitchen as you cook Thanksgiving dinner, never getting in your way, but automatically picking up and washing bowls and pots and utensils as you finish with them (but never prematurely), so there's always a clean one handy when you need it, you'll see why we found Java so attractive as a language and wanted it so badly. I didn't care about its alleged support for multiple platforms; I wanted it for writing better Windows applications more quickly.

Responding to that desire, Microsoft developed a set of Java tools called J++ that ran on Windows. J++ offered two choices: Using it in the classic, Sun-defined way, programmers could write a "pure" Java program that they could at least try to run on other platforms, and which might, after a lot of fiddling, totter to its feet on some of them. Or programmers could throw a switch in J++ that would make their programs easier and faster to write by allowing programmers to directly use certain pieces of the Windows operating system that didn't exist on other platforms, such as Object Linking and Embedding. We still had that great memory cleanup feature, known as "garbage collection," and most of the other features we liked about the Java language. The snag was that programs written in this way would run only on Windows and not on other platforms, since the pieces of Windows that they had come to depend on weren't available on those other platforms. If I thought that finishing the Windows version of my program sooner would make me more money, I could choose the Microsoft way. If I thought that taking longer to complete the Windows version but also covering the Macintosh and UNIX markets when I did so was a better bet, I could choose Sun's way.

Sun didn't like the idea of me having that choice. They screamed that this was evil and filed suit against Microsoft to stop it, calling it a "polluted" version of Java. Call it what you like, it was a choice that programmers hadn't had before. Sun claimed that programmers didn't realize what J++ was doing to our applications. We knew damn well. We're geeks; we're smart, remember? We chose it deliberately because the success of almost all software development projects depends on getting to market sooner than their competitors. And a program written in J++ for Windows only would get to market sooner than one written in J++ for all platforms, and much sooner than one written in C++.

As with most lawsuits, this one was settled. In 2001, Microsoft paid a few million dollars (a week or two of Jennifer Gates' allowance, probably less than Sun had spent on legal bills) and agreed to stop using the "J" word. Microsoft has since created their own Java-like language, called C# ("see-sharp"; think of it as two ++ signs stacked on top of each other and leaning forward as if in motion), which builds only Windows applications. That's where I spend most of my programming time, and I find it superior to the coffee language. When I talk about java now, I mean the stuff I drink to stay awake during long nights of programming in C#. At least until Sun sues me to call my caffeinated beverage something else.

You can't help but feel at least a little bit sorry for Microsoft here. On the one hand, the DOJ threatens to vivisect them for allegedly not providing enough choice. On the other hand, at more or less the same time, Sun whacks them for allegedly providing too much choice. And both lawsuits wind up costing them significant time and money. I think this is why the phrase "can't win for losing" was coined.

A Microsoft tech-support guy gets drafted into the army and sent to basic training. On the rifle range, he takes a few shots and misses the target every time. "You maggot," shouts the drill instructor, kicking him in the ribs. "You couldn't hit the broad side of a barn." The Microsoft tech-support guy puts his finger over the muzzle of the rifle, pulls the trigger with his other hand, and blam! He blows the end off his finger. "Well, it's leaving here OK," he says, pointing downrange with the bloody stump. "The problem must be on their end."

WE LOVE TO HATE THEM

Good scapegoats are valuable. We all need somebody on who to blame the latest snowstorm or a spouse's low libido or the new surfing control software at work blocking our favorite, er, recreational Web sites. In his classic *Travels with Charley*, John Steinbeck writes of an encounter in Minnesota, where a man tells him how the locally preferred scapegoat had changed from domestic to foreign. " 'Why, I remember when people took everything out on Mr. Roosevelt. Andy Larsen got red in the face about Roosevelt when his hens got the croup. Yes, sir,' he said with growing enthusiasm, 'those Russians got quite a load to carry. Man has a fight with his wife, he belts the Russians.' " To which Steinbeck replies, "Maybe everybody needs Russians. I'll bet even in Russia they need Russians. Maybe they call it Americans."

Would the jokes in this chapter be as funny if you downloaded a patch for Oracle brand condoms, or if the guy shooting the end off his finger was a Chevrolet mechanic? No. That tells you that there's something special about our relationship with Microsoft. Whenever I need a laugh line in one of my talks, I tell a Microsoft joke, and it never fails as long as I don't blow the delivery, sort of like a mother-in-law joke.[10]

The ubiquity of Windows means that something from Microsoft has probably pissed us off within the last few hours, in a way that other giant companies such as ExxonMobil or Citibank probably haven't. Even if the program that crashed and lost our last two weeks' worth of work wasn't written by Microsoft, the annoyance still took place on Windows, and we tend to chalk it up to Microsoft's account even if it doesn't belong there.

Some people carry it to extremes, making hatred for Microsoft the centerpiece of their personalities, if that's what you

---

10. Can you remember who we got annoyed at before Microsoft, back in the late '80s or so? I think it might have been the Japanese, buying Rockefeller Center with the money they got selling lots of imported cars. And before that it was big oil companies raising the price of gas to over a dollar per gallon.

want to call them. I remember once giving a presentation with two other top authors of books on Microsoft system programming at a bookstore in San Jose, California. To Microsoft, this Silicon Valley area is the belly of the beast. Sun Microsystems is next door in Los Gatos, Apple Computer up the road in Cupertino, what's left of Netscape a little farther up in Mountain View, Oracle over in Redwood Shores, Yahoo! and Google nearby. We figured that if our book tour could make it there, we could make it anywhere, and we pretty much filled the Barnes & Noble. During question time, one guy apparently became infatuated with his hatred for Microsoft and his love for his own voice, saying something like (my own paraphrase, I don't have his exact words anymore): "My question is, since Microsoft is an evil monopoly, when an evil monopoly does monopolistic, evil things like Microsoft, that evil monopoly, because they are a monopoly and they are evil…" I finally had to break in and say, "Is there a question here somewhere? Because so far it's a speech, and I'll make the speeches here, thank you. Next questioner—you there, sir."

Boston Globe columnist Hiawatha Bray, whose viewpoint I've always found to be even-handed, has discussed this tendency. In 2004, he wrote:

"There's something about Microsoft Corp. that makes smart people stupid…. [T]he aura of arrogant, absolute power emanating from the world's biggest software maker … drives some people into a blind fury, a determination to hurt Microsoft, no matter the cost to consumers or the software industry."

He cites as an example the European Community's antitrust commission attempting to make Microsoft remove their music and video player, named Windows Media Player, from Windows. Exactly how removing the operating system's ability to play music would benefit consumers, how plugging in your brand-new computer and discovering that it couldn't play music, would make you happier than if it could, I don't quite see, but let that pass for now. Microsoft offered a compromise in which Media Player would stay, but Microsoft would also install arch-rival Real Player and a player-to-be-named-later.[11]

Bray continues: "Any government official who simply wanted to improve the lot of Microsoft users would have leaped from his seat and kissed [Microsoft CEO Steve] Ballmer on both cheeks. You want real competition in media players? You got it. But the EU rejected the compromise, probably for the same reason that so many others have snubbed compromise with Microsoft. They don't just want a deal that's good for the public, and even for other software companies. They want to hurt Microsoft, make it suffer, wipe that smug, know-it-all grin off Bill Gates' billionaire face."

I've said for many years that Microsoft doesn't have just a technical job to do, but also a public relations job. They're not doing nearly as good a job on the latter as they are on the former because they don't seem to realize its importance. For example, in 2001, Microsoft announced a service offering one worldwide login, one highly secured location for a user's personal data such as calendars and credit cards, and access to that data from anywhere in the world using any platform or Web-enabled device. It had some useful features and some not so useful, and might or might not have succeeded on its own merits. However, any technical merit that it might have possessed became irrelevant when Microsoft gave it the colossally dumb name of "Hailstorm." It was only an internal code name, but it quickly escaped, triggered all kinds of evil empire associations, and unleashed a firestorm of criticism, similar to the FBI naming their e-mail scanning program "Carnivore." Microsoft pulled the plug on it about a year later. Naming it something like "At Your Service" would have put a completely different spin on it and probably would have kept the mainstream press from piling on, as the FBI should have named their program something like "Staunch Defender."

---

11. Sorry, I couldn't resist, but it's true. There was to be a third player installed, and the choice of it was to be made by the system vendor at a later time.

Since geeks judge one another on their brains, it seldom occurs to them that nongeeks might use a different yardstick. It shouldn't surprise anyone that a company founded and run by geeks is lacking in the social graces, but Microsoft has reached the point where their social ineptitude is hurting their bottom line. "But we're good people here," they say to me. "Look at all the money we just gave to disaster relief. What do you mean people don't like us? Of course they do. It's just a few jealous nuts who don't. After all, we like us, and everyone else is just like us, right?"

Listen, Microsoft—how many times have I said it in this book? Your. User. Is. Not. You. All the spin in the world won't make a bad product good or even mediocre. But the best technical product in the world is useless if you don't understand your users, if you've solved the wrong problem or solved the right one in a way that your users can't swallow. It doesn't matter what you think your customers think, or wish they thought. You have to deal with what they do think. You can't continue to be, as has often been said, five square miles of Redmond surrounded by reality. It can be done, once you face the fact that it has to be. Look at Johnson & Johnson, which has always been one of the world's most respected companies, despite seven people dying in 1982 when an unknown criminal tampered with their Tylenol pain reliever on drugstore shelves. Microsoft software hasn't killed anyone yet, at least not that I'm aware of. If J&J can pull it off in the face of multiple random and horrible deaths, so can you in the face of much less adversity. It'll require growing up, though, and that's always painful.

These are real instructions. Run Minesweeper from your Start menu and wait until it appears on the screen. Then, with three fingers of your left hand, simultaneously hold down the left-hand Ctrl, the left-hand Alt, and the left-hand Shift keys. While you are holding down these three keys, type the five characters XYZZY with your right hand. Then release all the left-hand keys. Now press and release the left-hand Shift key only. You have turned on a hidden mine detector. Move the mouse over any square in the Minesweeper game, hidden or

FIGURE 8-3 Turning on this mine detector means that you don't need to play the game ever again.

revealed. *If that square does not contain a mine, the upper-left dot of your desktop screen (not the Minesweeper window, the entire desktop screen; you may have to move other windows to see it) will turn white (see Figure 8–3). If you move the mouse over a square containing a mine, the dot will turn black. What's the joke in this paragraph? Well, I've just ruined Minesweeper for you. Now that you know how to beat it every time, there's no reason to play it anymore, is there? I just boosted your productivity, now and in the future. You're welcome. No extra charge. And don't annoy me or I'll tell you the Solitaire cheat codes and really ruin your life.*

PLUS ÇA CHANGE

Anyone either bashing or wanting to influence Microsoft has to keep in mind the constraints which bind Microsoft. As you once thought of your parents as omnipotent, as my daughters (six and three years old) currently think me (bless them), it's easy to overlook those constraints. But think of the United States, often called the world's only superpower, currently swatting a swarm of pesky hornets. We could crush them if they'd just hold still, but they know this, so they keep moving. When you say, "Why don't those [exple-tives] at Microsoft do [this] or stop doing [that]," you need to under-stand that they labor under at least four constraints that aren't immediately obvious to the casual observer.

First, their new products, and especially changes to their exist-ing products, are constrained to a surprising degree by their base of existing users. It is very difficult to release a new product that breaks something users are used to doing. "How did God manage to create the world in only six days?" goes the old geek joke. The answer is that "He didn't have any installed base to worry about backward compatibility with."

For example, consider an old feature called DDE, for Dynamic Data Exchange. First released in Microsoft's Excel spreadsheet program around 1988, it was the first technology that allowed data to be automatically piped from one Windows applica-tion to another without a human user touching it. It was the greatest thing since sliced bread when it first came out, and I remember sell-ing a big project to a customer by demonstrating it. It was super-seded around 1993 by a technology called OLE (those TLAs again, see Chapter 7); more reliable and easier to program properly once you'd gotten your head around it. But so many users, particularly in the financial industry, had by then written Excel spreadsheets that depended on DDE that Microsoft can't get rid of it. These users would consider a release without it to be a downgrade rather than an upgrade, and you can understand their reluctance to pay money for downgrades. To this day, financial market data vendor Bloomberg continues to supply its online stock quotes in this format, alongside other newer ones. When Microsoft adds new features to Excel or beefs up its security or even fiddles with its internals in any way, they have to make sure they don't break DDE. It's like sex—one moment of unguarded geeky feature-passion that feels great at the time, and you have to support the result for the next 20 years, sometimes longer. Multiply this trouble by all the other obsolete features and it gets damned expensive.

The second constraint is the unbelievable diversity of software and hardware environments that Windows and Windows applications have to run on. Windows computers vary far more than you think: processor speed, memory sizes, installed hardware such as printers and mice and networks and sound cards, and the other programs running at the same time. Like snowflakes, essentially no two of the hundreds of millions of PCs running in the world are alike. Apple restricted this diversity in their universe by tightly controlling the Macintosh computer hardware, and their computers are more reliable as a result. But users didn't reward Apple for that reliability by buying very many of them. Regardless of what their voices might have said, consumers said with their purchasing dollars that they valued the lower prices and possibly the greater flexibility of Windows, by a factor of 20 to 1.

No matter how carefully any manufacturer tests their products, when you install a program on your PC that is almost certainly the first moment in the history of the universe in which that program encountered that exact computing environment. The miracle is that most software more or less works, most of the time. It's very, very hard to reproduce bugs in a Windows environment. Now that Windows contains a crash recorder, which I'll explain later in this chapter, we can see exactly what an application was doing when it died. This constraint is getting smaller.

Third, this diversity and its attendant problems apply to the user population as well. What's good and right and necessary for one class of users may be entirely wrong for a different class of users. Consider the mutual fund company Vanguard, which manages almost a trillion dollars of customer assets, a tiny fraction of which is mine. Their networks receive many, many attacks (a different financial company once told me that his company's main Web site got more than a hundred attacks *per second*), and the cost of a breach could be huge. Vanguard's need for security is enormous, which they realize, and they spend lots of money to deal with it. For example, their employees who use PCs are generally not allowed to install software on their own machines, or receive e-mail from external providers such as Yahoo! and Hotmail. An army of trained professionals is in charge of deciding which applications are safe and installing them for the people who need them. Solitaire tends to be frowned on in this sort of place, and forget about Star Trek games. All this security makes their computers harder to use, but that's a trade-off they are forced to make because of the business they are in. Because the monetary rewards are higher, the users' hassle budget (see Chapter 3) is much higher. They will put up with much more hassle to avoid trouble because they have to.

Ordinary home users, on the other hand, don't get anywhere near that number of attacks and the cost of a security breach is much less. They use their computers for tasks much more diverse than office jobs. They can't and won't spend anywhere near the amount of effort to keep themselves safe. The balance between usability and security has to shift toward the former, compared to what's appropriate at a mutual fund company. A home user's hassle budget is much lower. Windows XP has to be secure enough for the mutual fund company, while simultaneously being easy enough for a home user to install and use. It's a very difficult balancing act, and I sometimes wonder how long one product will be able to serve both markets.

Finally, you need to remember that the cost of Windows is very low, and that means you don't get much handholding. The cost of Windows XP Home is about $90 if you buy it separately on Amazon.com. Most users get their operating systems preinstalled when they buy a PC, in which case it costs much less. Dell is currently selling a home PC with decent functionality (adequate memory, reasonable hard drive, network adapter, sound card, some software, even a 17-inch monitor; the works, really) running Windows XP Home for $299. You can't get a whole lot of handholding for that price.

Three women are comparing their husbands' performance in bed. The first one says, "My husband's an opera singer, and he always serenades me. It's wonderful." The second says, *"My husband's a policeman, and he likes me to wear handcuffs. I've actually gotten to like it. How about yours?"* The third lady blushes a little and says, *"Well, my husband works for Microsoft, and we never actually do anything. He just sits there on the edge of the bed showing me a PowerPoint presentation, promising how great it's going to be when he finally gets it up and running."*

GROWING-UP PAINS

In my never-ending quest for free food and drink, I recently crashed a dinner party thrown by Microsoft's medical industry consulting practice. The atmosphere felt strange, uncomfortable, alien, and I couldn't put my finger on why. It wasn't the easy camaraderie of top programmers or Tech Ed speakers, guys I've known on and off over the years, where we've read each other's books and articles and share many mutual acquaintances. I tried a few of the usual geek conversation openers ("Have you heard how much the memory garbage collection algorithms have changed from version 1.1 to version 2?"), but the blank stares I got in return told me that we weren't speaking the same language.

"Plattski, this is the New Microsoft," said the friend who had invited me, a renegade physician whom I had taught to program many years ago.[12] "You and I are some of the last of the old ones. Look here, we've got workflow consultants, regulatory specialists, clinicians, salespeople, but essentially no programmers, except that guy over there in the corner crying into his beer and mumbling to himself. We're dinosaurs, like the ones in the billboard ads who won't upgrade their copy of Office. How the hell did that happen?"

Microsoft started out as, and pretty much remains, a product-driven company. By this I mean that their programmers develop an

---

12. He may join me as a co-author of *Why Medicine Sucks* when I finish the sequel to this book, *Why Software STILL Sucks.*

operating system, then throw it over the fence to the user community and go off to build the next one, like an obstetrician delivering a baby and handing it off to the parents. The difference is that this baby was designed by the obstetrician from pure thought-stuff and is unlike anything ever seen on the planet before. The new parents don't have a million years of evolution guiding their instincts with the new operating system, and asking their own parents what they did when they got handed one ("read the manual and prayed a lot") probably won't be helpful. The person who knows the new baby best, the obstetrician, has gone back to his lab to whip up the next baby, probably with a lot of ideas from the first one that he hadn't had time to implement, and isn't all that interested in how the first one fares, especially since he wants the new one to replace it in a couple of years, as soon as he gets it done. The people that deal with customers using the new baby, "technical evangelists," Microsoft calls them, had minimal pull on the product teams. That's starting to change now, as Microsoft realizes that a) they can't just throw out new products and expect people to buy them, and b) ongoing support and consulting services can be highly profitable, as they are for IBM.

Microsoft was founded in 1975. They were about ten years old when they first released Windows, 15 years old when Windows started taking off, just over 30 as I write this book. Think of yourself at age 15, and again at age 30. When you were 15, you just wanted to do stuff that you thought was cool and fun. Responsibility wasn't high on your list, except for the minimum you had to show (or at least fake) to get use of the family car (see cool and fun stuff). It shouldn't surprise anyone that Microsoft, at age 15, placed a high value on doing programming stuff that they considered cool and fun, aided by the fact that they could make a hell of a lot of money doing it, with which money they could do even more cool and fun stuff. That's how we got things like Easter eggs[13] in Excel.

---

13. An Easter egg is a hidden piece of a program put in by programmers for the fun of it. The Minesweeper cheat sequence that I describe earlier in this chapter is a form of Easter egg. Excel was especially famous for elaborate Easter eggs.

Microsoft operating systems didn't run hospitals or air traffic control systems in 1990, as teenagers shouldn't. They claimed that they were ready to, as teenagers always do, but as one current Microsoft employee describes those days, "We suffered from delusions of adequacy." Microsoft is just now gaining traction in such projects, as 30-year-olds should. The entire industry has matured, has had to mature. As Steve Ballmer wrote in a 2002 e-mail: "...even five years ago, we still tended to think of ourselves as the small startup company that we were not so long ago. Today we recognize that our decisions have an impact on many other technology companies. We have an important leadership role to play in our industry, and we must play by new rules—both legally and as determined by industry trends." It takes a while, and it's not without its false starts and blind alleys, but they're moving in that direction rather than the opposite one. Microsoft hires more lawyers today, and fewer geeks. They're more responsible and less fun; like a kitten becoming a cat. It has to be that way if they're to run the world—you don't want a 15-year-old with a playful sense of humor running a nuclear missile submarine ("Hey, what does this button do? Oops!"). But often, as I'm struggling with their internal bureaucracy over this or that arcane regulation, I fondly remember the old shoot-from-the-hip, ready-fire-aim days, as I fondly remember (at least partially) my teen years.

Google is now in its adolescent days, the way Microsoft was then. Google has more fun, partly because they have less responsibility. Sure, I recommend Google and use them all the time, but if they disappeared tomorrow, I'd survive—Yahoo!, MSN Search, Alta Vista, or Lycos would more or less get my searching work done. It'd be much harder to do that if Microsoft disappeared.

A shepherd was tending his flock one day when a Range Rover sporting a satellite dish on its roof drove over the meadow and stopped next to him. Out jumped a business-suited yuppie with a tablet PC. "Excuse me, my good man," said the newcomer. "If I can tell you how many sheep you have, will you give me one of them?" The shepherd nods assent. The man scribbles on the PC screen, writing a program that accesses real-time satellite photographs of the meadow, counting the shadows thrown by the sheep's legs and dividing by four. "You have exactly 197 sheep, counting that three-legged one over there, is that correct?" The shepherd nods again, so the man selects an animal and starts getting back in his SUV. The shepherd now speaks his first words: "You work for Microsoft, don't you?" "Why yes, how did you know?" "You came here uninvited, charging me an outrageous fee for an answer I already knew to a question I hadn't asked. And you don't know squat about my business." "What!?" huffs the yuppie, purpling with rage. "Microsoft is the worldwide software leader. Our software is on 97 percent of the PCs in the world, and half the servers. Our chairman is the richest man in the world. How can an uncouth yokel like you tell a double Ph.D. like me that we don't understand your business?" The shepherd replies, "Put the dog down, and I'll explain it to you."

WHAT YOU CAN DO ABOUT IT

As I've said throughout this book, vendors won't supply better software until users start demanding it. "When people tell us that something sucks, we start making it better," a Microsoft evangelist recently told me when I discussed this book with him over breakfast in Iceland. "It's just much more difficult than you'd imagine for us to know what sucks and what doesn't."

The *New Orleans Times-Picayune*, demanding Category 5 levees in the wake of Hurricane Katrina, told its readers to write their legislators. "Flood them with mail the way we were flooded by Katrina," the paper said. That's the first thing users need to do with Microsoft, or any other software vendor. Again, you need to be as specific as possible. Just shouting "you suck," no matter how good it makes you feel, doesn't tell a vendor what it is that you don't like. Try to compose yourself. "We like this. We don't like that. We really need such-and-such, but this thing here just gets in our way." And don't be too surprised if they don't take your advice immediately, or even ever. The user population of a mass-market application like, say, Excel, is enormous, and it's extremely difficult to balance the demands of different types of users. You may think that a feature is a complete waste of time, even counterproductive, but someone else might use it all day, every day. The eternal paradox, of course, is how any software vendor can learn what the "silent majority" of users think. By definition, they don't say much.

You can see an example of this flood of mail bringing results in the first week of January 2006. A security reviewer discovered a new vulnerability in Internet Explorer called the Windows Metafile hole. Microsoft produced a patch to fix it, but didn't want to release it until their regular update release the following week, wanting time to test it more, as we've seen how they have to support it forever once it goes out the door. Microsoft didn't consider this vulnerability critical because they said that most antivirus programs were catching the infected files. The user community clearly disagreed. Security-related boards and mailing lists carried a hailstorm of criticism. A Russian developer produced a patch that was thought to fix the hole, and a number of respected security authorities endorsed it and recommended users install it immediately instead of waiting for Microsoft's patch. The widespread publicity, and the thought of having to support browsers with a third-party patch, caused Microsoft to advance their schedule, test around the clock, and release their patch immediately.

Without taking sides as to whether this bug was or wasn't serious enough to advance the release schedule, the user community clearly felt that it was, and Microsoft didn't understand the depth of that feeling. So they got a black eye, similar to the one Intel got years ago when it came to light that their Pentium chips had tiny math errors in high decimal places, and Intel waffled and tried to ignore it instead of dealing forthrightly with their customers. (*Q: What's 665.99999999999842? A: The number of the beast on a Pentium, but that's close enough for you nonscientific users.*) The public pressure did it. If Microsoft had done a *mea culpa* à la Johnson & Johnson, it would have blown over quickly, but trying to brush it off merely amplified its perceived importance.

Go ahead, try non-Microsoft applications. Download a free trial of WordPerfect from Corel. Try the Firefox Web browser. I can't stand it, popping message boxes into my face to signal errors, but some people swear by it. (I swear at it, but maybe that's just me.) If nothing else, its presence has forced Microsoft to update their plans for the next version of Internet Explorer.

Want to ditch Microsoft entirely? It can be done. Tony Bove's book, *Just Say No to Microsoft: How to Ditch Microsoft and Why It's Not as Hard as You Think* (No Starch Press, 2005), purports to explain how. The fact that it's currently ranked #265,413 in sales on Amazon.com would seem to indicate that not many users put a high value on a Microsoft-free life for its own sake. It illustrates yet again—from the other side this time—that most users don't care about their tools, only their results. Home Depot might think they're in the business of selling drills, but customers go to Home Depot because they want holes.

One thing that nobody likes, other than consultants like me that make a living from them, is a crash—when a program falls over dead or freezes completely for no apparent reason. The most recent versions of Microsoft products have therefore contained a "crash recorder" conceptually similar to the black boxes used on aircraft. You've probably seen it working, as shown in Figure 8–4. It means that an error from deep down inside one program (maybe the program, maybe the operating system or its add-ons) has happened and the application wasn't able to handle it and keep going. Back in Windows 3.0 and earlier, the entire box used to freeze with an "Unrecoverable Application Error," and you had to turn the power off and try again. Windows NT was usually able to shut down just the offending application and keep everything else going, although not always—remember our old friend, the Blue Screen of Death (see Figure 8–5), when NT lost its mind? Even if

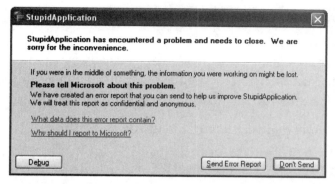

FIGURE 8-4 The crash recorder asking permission to send the report to Microsoft

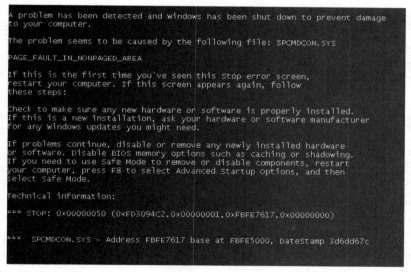

FIGURE 8-5 Windows XP blue screen of death

NT stayed up, we generally didn't get any information about the crash, nothing that would keep it from happening again. Now, Windows XP almost always stays alive, and the crash recorder takes a snapshot of the dead program and sends it to Microsoft for analysis. This report tells them, among other things, the exact line of the program at which the error took place and all the layers that it worked its way up through.

I can't overemphasize just how useful this automatic crash reporting is to a development team. In my early programming days, our support line would get calls like this:

> Client: "*Ah, I think something's wrong with my program.*"
> Me: "*What are the symptoms?*"
> Client: "*I don't know. It just sort of didn't work in a funny kind of way.*"
> Me: "*What were you doing with it at the time?*"
> Client: "*Can't remember, just sort of using it and stuff.*"
> Me: "*Have you had this before?*"
> Client: "*Yes.*"
> Me: "*Well, you've got it again. That's all I can tell you. Goodbye (click).*"

These reports didn't tell us much except that the program was rickety, which I assure you we already knew. But we didn't know how or where, which made it impossible to figure out why. I've seen more than one company killed by their inability to debug applications like this. Bugs often depend heavily on timing or other programs in the system, conditions impossible to reproduce outside the customer's machine.

As Steve Ballmer wrote in a published e-mail: "We've been amazed by the patterns revealed in the error reports that customers are sending us. The reports identify bugs not only in our own software, but in Windows-based applications from independent hardware and software vendors as well. One really exciting thing we learned is how, among all the software bugs involved in reports, a relatively small proportion causes most of the errors. About 20 percent of the bugs cause 80 percent of all errors, and—this is stunning to me—one percent of bugs cause half of all errors." I think that if I were a software vendor and had Ballmer banging on my desk, waving a bug report in my face, shouting, *"It's this line right here, you idoit!"* I'd give a high priority to fixing it.

The main worry that users have with the crash recorder is that its report sometimes contains data from the document they were working on when the crash happened, and this data might be sensitive. A U.S. Department of Energy bulletin[14] describes this possibility, reports that the document's data appears in the crash report about one time in three, and recommends that users disable this feature. Microsoft's crash recorder privacy policy swears that they will use the data only for good and never for evil. Nevertheless, the policy states that "Microsoft employees, contractors, and vendors who have a business need to use the error report data are provided access. If the error report indicates that a third-party product is involved, Microsoft may send the data to the vendor of that product, who may in turn send the data to sub-vendors and partners." In other words, whatever cat was in the bag when your program crashed could easily come out, so in high-confidentiality applications I'd turn it off.[15] Still, if you want the doctor to be able to fix your condition, you have to tell him where it hurts, and probably also show him. And like your doctor, I guarantee that whatever embarrassing thing you were doing when the crash hit, they've seen it a thousand times before, almost certainly to the point of boredom. (Ah, that deadly *almost*.)

You see again how Microsoft sometimes gets stuck in the middle. If they don't get crash recorder data, they'll never fix the bugs or even detect them. On the other hand, if they do get sent this data, then users get mad about their confidentiality being violated. I hope that enough nonsensitive users leave the reporting turned on that Microsoft can learn enough to fix the damn thing. I leave my error reporting turned on, unless a client requires otherwise in a contract

---

14. Currently online at www.ciac.org/ciac/bulletins/m-005.shtml.

15. Open the Control Panel and select System. Then select the Advanced tab. In the lower right-hand corner, click the Error Reporting button. Select the radio button labeled Disable Error Reporting.

and pays for my extra hassle. I figure it's like in *The Godfather* by Mario Puzo, when the drug dealer Sollozzo kidnaps Corleone family *consigliore* Tom Hagen. He says: "Get in the car. If I wanted to kill you you'd be dead now."

There is a hysterical video now on the Web, apparently produced by Microsoft's European office. It shows Microsoft's "We Share Your Pain," or WSYP (pronounced "WIZ-zip"), program extending the crash recorder's capabilities so that it identifies the developer who wrote the specific piece of code that failed and offers users the chance to express their frustrations by remotely jabbing him with a needle or applying electric shock. "Microsoft has got the best programmers, we hope. And this program will help them to share, understand, the users in a very direct way," says one of the characters. I've found it several times on the Microsoft Web site, but it moves around, so I can't give you a definitive URL in this book. Your favorite search engine will point you at it very quickly, and I'll attempt to keep a link to it on this book's Web site. It could be that they're actually listening to me when I say, "Know thy user."

> Q: *How many Microsoft tech-support guys does it take to change a light bulb?*
> A: *I'm afraid we can't reproduce your problem. All the light bulbs here are working fine.*

THE LAST WORD

The late advice columnist, Ann Landers (1918–2002), used to boil any question about husbands or boyfriends down to a single bit: "Well, honey, are you better off with him or without him?" I invite you to answer that question for yourself about Microsoft. Imagine snapping your fingers and everything in the world built by Microsoft magically vanishes. Is the world a better place or a worse one? Not everyone agrees with me, but I say the latter. So I hope they don't. And so do my creditors.

My grandmother, 40 years ago, used to say when I'd complain about a bad telephone connection, "I remember when we didn't have telephones at all. Now you can pick up the phone and call me anytime. Do you think a grandmother likes that? It's a whole lot better than we had before, which was nothing at all." I can't remember back to no computers at all, but I can remember when a computer was this gargantuan thing the size of a Winnebago in an air-conditioned glass house, used only by the Social Security Administration and the IRS, and had less computing power than your toothbrush does today. Thirty years ago, we had minicomputers from DEC the size of a refrigerator or two, still in glass houses (smaller, but still air-conditioned), which colleges could afford if they had lots of rich alumni with bad hearts. Twenty years ago we got the first personal computers, IBM and Apple putting computing power on individual desktops. Ten years ago Windows started letting you play Solitaire while checking e-mail on your dial-up modem. Now it's XP and the Web, where crashes get reported and updates downloaded automatically. Tell me life isn't getting better and better. Remember where we were, and how far we've come, is what my grandmother would tell me if she was alive and could understand it. So I'll tell you on her behalf.

Bill Gates finally dies, and with such a checkered past, St. Peter can't decide whether he ought to go up or down. So he offers Bill his choice of heaven or hell. Naturally Bill wants to look them over before picking a place to spend eternity, so he visits them both. Heaven's OK; the angel wings are kinda cool, but it's pretty tame compared to what he's used to. Down in hell, he sees wild parties on the beach, rivers of beer, mountains of food, nonstop bands and dancing girls, Xbox video console shoot-'em-up game tournaments, all kinds of great stuff. So he chooses hell. As soon as the door slams with him inside, he's engulfed in burning hellfire, smothered with brimstone, surrounded by screaming devils that all look like Janet Reno jabbing him with pitchforks, all kinds of awful torment. "Wait!" he e-mails Satan from the 300-baud modem in his Commodore 64, the only computer available (more torture). "What happened to the parties? The booze? The dancing girls? The Xboxes?" "Surely, Mr. Gates," replies the Prince of Darkness, "you of all people should understand the difference between the demo version and the finished product."

9

. . .

DOING SOMETHING ABOUT IT

The software industry exists because of you, the user. Developers sometimes forget that, and some of them never quite got it through their heads in the first place, but that's their ultimate goal: to write programs that you like and will therefore buy or Web sites that you like and will therefore use, thus rewarding those developers and their employers.

As any recovering alcoholic will tell you, the first step in any recovery is admitting that a problem exists. Many programmers need to do that. ("My name is Bob, and I write software that sucks." "Hi, Bob.") Sometimes they come to this realization on their own ("Holy Toledo, did I really write that piece of crap?"), but more often they need intervention. ("Bob, do you have any idea how stupid this Web site is that you designed for us? You make the user think five separate times before he can even begin doing the work he came here to do. Nobody's completed the process even once since the site went live, although five thousand have started and given up halfway through. And it wouldn't have happened if you'd read Plattski's book.") That's where you come in.

You're not a programmer and don't want to be one, but you have valuable, nay, *invaluable*, contributions to make in improving software. Developers need you to tell them what you need and what you want, what you love and what you hate, what you hope for and what you fear. They can't know that on their own, even though they think they already do. Substituting their own values because they don't know yours leads them into damnation, as I hope you've seen by now.

As the aforementioned alcoholic will also tell you, the second step to recovery is to believe that a solution is possible. I've tried hard in this book to show you good examples (Google automatically detecting your country with exactly zero effort on your part) alongside bad ones (UPS.com making you choose your country with many mouse clicks, and then explicitly tell them whether you want them to remember it so that you don't have to go through that foolishness the next time), to demonstrate that good software not only is possible, but really does exist, at least occasionally. When programmers get it wrong, it's almost always because they don't understand what their users want and need and are willing to tolerate. This chapter focuses on providing developers with the feedback they need—how you go about telling them what kind of job they're doing for you, and how they need to do a better one. Here are five separate steps for you to take, which I call Plattski's Handful.

1. BUY

The first way in which consumers, of software or anything else, make their preferences known is through the products and services they buy and don't buy. Cars didn't improve until consumers started demanding that they do so, buying the reliable Toyotas and Hondas and leaving the rickety Pintos and Novas to rust on dealers' lots. As Lee Iacocca used to say in TV commercials for a then-resurgent Chrysler: "If you can find a better car, buy it." We did. And all cars got better as a result.

Software won't improve until the vendors feel our preferences in their wallets. Google became a powerhouse, dominating Yahoo!

and Microsoft in the Web search arena, because they provided a better search engine with a cleaner, easier user interface. Users rewarded them by using their search engine rather than the competition's. The users didn't pay Google directly, but their clicks on interesting advertisements caused advertisers (including myself) to do so. Lots of clicks. Lots of money. Big, profitable Google, because they got it right.

Money speaks louder than words. You may think and say with your voice that Macintosh computers are more reliable, or better designed, or just generally better than Windows PCs. You might even be right. But when you add it all up, not that many people buy them. The aggregate consumer preference is for Windows, by about 20 to 1. That tells Microsoft, in the only way that matters to them, that most people think they're doing things more or less right. If that ratio started to change significantly, you'd find Microsoft stepping hard on the gas to keep up. If your money's not behind it, don't be surprised if no one pays much attention to your mouth.

You can see a good example of competition changing even Microsoft's behavior in the current Web browser wars. Microsoft's Internet Explorer version 6, which comes installed on Windows, is more than five years old; ancient as the Internet reckons time. Other Web browser programs, such as Firefox (which gets the most press; but Opera and Safari are also gaining market share), offer useful features that Internet Explorer doesn't and are more secure besides. And when I say useful features, I mean things that real users really like; not useless doodads like floating menus and dancing paper-clips—features like a browser holding more than one page at a time, allowing you to switch between them using the tabs at the top of the screen, as shown in Figure 9–1. Like Internet Explorer, these browsers are also free, but users have to download them because they don't come preinstalled on Windows. They've caused Microsoft's share of the Web browser market to fall from 95 percent to about 85 percent, according to David Pogue of the *New York*

FIGURE 9-1 Firefox Web browser holding three separate pages at once. See the tabs just above the page window.

Times.[1] That's how users tell Microsoft, "Hey, put more people to work improving Internet Explorer, because that's what we care about." Microsoft responded by accelerating their release of Internet Explorer version 7, now due toward the end of 2006 rather than a year or two later. It will contain most of the features that users like from the other browsers, and will be more secure than Internet Explorer 6. That's competition doing what it should do, forcing everyone to stay on their toes.

---

1. Good numbers for browser market share are hard to come by and depend on who does the study, how the questions are phrased, and whom you want to believe. But there is general agreement that Microsoft's share, although still dominant, has retreated somewhat. Of course, it couldn't have gotten all that much higher.

Don't like the word processor or spreadsheet in Microsoft Office? Dump it. A quick Google search for "Microsoft Office" and "alternatives" produces almost 9 million hits. WordPerfect from Corel is a full-featured word processor, the market leader back in the days before Windows. It contains features that Microsoft Word doesn't, such as converting documents to and from the popular Adobe PDF format, and it costs less. Star Office from Sun Microsystems is still cheaper, does still less, and allows anyone with a religious yearning for programs written in Java to satisfy that itch. OpenOffice, a collaborative effort, does even less but is free. IBM offers SmartSuite, containing the 1-2-3 spreadsheet that launched the PC revolution, which it got when it bought Lotus. All these programs read and write Microsoft Office documents. And they all have their own quirks and drawbacks; the head-slappers that make you scream "What the hell were they thinking," just as with Microsoft Word, but in different places. The threat of these applications is causing Microsoft to work hard at making Office 12 (their next version) into a compelling upgrade, which Office 11 definitely was not.[2] Maybe Microsoft will succeed with the next Office, maybe they won't, but it keeps everyone working hard. For myself, I've got Word dialed in the way I like it, automatically correcting my most common misspellings, such as typing "hte" rather than "the," and I won't change programs, or even upgrade, until someone, Microsoft or not, shows me a compelling reason to do so.

Detest Windows? Stop whining and buy a Macintosh. My mother uses one and so do many of my colleagues at Harvard. They

---

2. Office 11 is the one Microsoft advertised with nonupgrading users wearing plastic dinosaur heads to show their supposed backwardness. "Dinosaur" is a vicious insult in the geek vocabulary, second perhaps only to "stupid." But it didn't bother users, who ignored the product in droves. Hey, Microsoft: Your user isn't you. Their fears (breaking an installation that currently works, useless junk like dancing paperclips slowing down their computers so that they need to buy new ones) aren't yours (appearing out-of-date). Know thy user, for he is not thee. Then you might sell some upgrades.

say they love them. Don't want to spend the extra money for one? Buy a Dell PC that uses a free open source operating system such as Linux. They start at $239, including a refurbished 17-inch monitor, but you'll have to do more work to find and install and worry about the compatibility of applications for it. If you like buying furniture at Ikea, where you have to select the heavy boxes from the warehouse, schlep them to the cash register and then home, and assemble them yourself, in return for a lower price, you might like this idea. Don't have time or patience or strength for any of this nonsense? Maybe you like Windows more than you thought you did. Seems to me that it does a lot of good stuff for a hundred bucks, but not everyone agrees.

Crackpot world domination theorists aside, you have many choices in the software you buy. Don't automatically pick the program with the longest list of features, unless there's one that you just can't live without and that no other application has. Insist on a free trial, which almost all programs allow these days, and make sure you start it when you have some time to put a program through its paces. Run the software, try a few tasks in it, and make sure that it's easy to use. If it's not, dump it and find one that is. Your dollars provide an immediate reward to the good guys, and the lack of them punishes the bad.

If a company's Web site is bad, don't use it. Call their customer service lines instead and talk to a human, which costs them much more money. Get a speaker on your next phone, so you don't have to hold it to your ear while you wait for an agent. Or better still, take your money to a company with a good Web site, or at least a better one. A well-designed Web site improves everyone's life, but a poorly designed one costs both parties. An early reviewer of this book reports that for him, "The worst offender [at] making you fill out page after page of forms and then saying 'Server too busy; try again later' without saving anything is USAirways.com. They've done this to me repeatedly, to the point where I now book on other airlines whenever possible, and make USAir reservations by phone when necessary." That costs the company another $20 when he does fly with them, not to mention the lost business when he doesn't. Is it any wonder they're hemorrhaging money?

Buy the good stuff, or at least the better stuff, or at least the less bad stuff. That's the clearest message you can send.

2. TELL

Every successful business listens to its customers. I remember once as a boy, opening a box of Cheerios and finding many of them burnt. My parents helped me write a (relatively) polite letter to the address on the box. In a few days, I was rewarded with a response: a form letter apologizing, explaining what had happened, and most important, containing a coupon for two free boxes of Cheerios. I was thrilled to get them, and really annoyed when my parents made me share them with my little brother.

Most manufacturers *want* to hear from their customers. They understand that they need to know what their customers think, what they like and don't like, what they want to see change and what they want to see stay the same. As engineering professor Henry Petroski writes in *Success Through Failure: the Paradox of Design* (Princeton University Press, 2006): "Dissatisfied customers are the source of important feedback on designs to manufacturers. Indeed, they provide the kind of information that is not readily obtained in any other way, for designers and manufacturers are often too close to a product to fully appreciate all the ways in which it can fail to live up to its promise.... [Designers] develop myopia as they learn to massage and manipulate the device to avoid its shortcomings. They define its limits, and so test the product within them. Purchasers, however, seldom acknowledge such limits or read the fine print in the user's manual. No end of testing in a laboratory may ever uncover a flaw or weakness …that can be immediately recognized by an imaginative maven."

A few software makers and Web designers haven't read Petroski or Alan Cooper or this book, and think they can avoid listening to their users. They use the product all day, every day; they're the ones who know how it works, so they're the ones who know what's important. As I've shown you throughout this book, that's dead wrong. Fortunately, most developers are smart enough to realize that they need your input. They want to sell more products or have you visit their Web site more often, so if you send them polite comments, they'll appreciate it far more often than not. This doesn't mean they'll put in every feature that anyone ever asks for. You might want something that's impossible, or something that would break other things, or the way you personally think might be ass-backwards compared to what other users think. But developers prioritize items in response to the sum total of their customer feedback. In particular, fixes to the problems that generate the most tech-support calls (very expensive, as I've shown you) get a high priority. So call them frequently when something breaks.

Companies need to read their mail, although you might not think so by the difficulties that they put in the way of your sending feedback forms, like UPS.com that I discussed in Chapter 2. UPS requires you to work your way through five levels of forms, and then fill out seven separate entries to send them e-mail. To make sending feedback easier for you, I've put a direct link to this page on this book's Web site, www.whysoftwaresucks.com. And I've done that for some of the other companies that I've lambasted, like Starbucks. I'll try to keep these links up-to-date. And I'll add others as you tell me about them. We'll make this a movement yet, as I describe at the end of this chapter.

User feedback has the most influence on a product during its earliest public testing, often called "beta testing." For example, Microsoft just completed beta testing of its new OneCare product, an online subscription service that purports to keep your computer safe. I found its functionality underwhelming compared to market leaders Norton and McAfee, but perhaps its ease of use will make up for this. Thousands of users participated in this test, in which we installed early versions of this software on our computers, tried it out, and gave feedback. Microsoft provided an Internet bulletin board on which users could report their experiences, give their opinions, ask questions, and get Microsoft's answers. In this particular trial, repeated requests from users led to the substantial improvement of its file backup capability.

Microsoft started beta testing the aforementioned Internet Explorer version 7 just as this book went to press. They announced it on their home page, www.microsoft.com, and allowed any interested user to join. You can find other beta tests if you look around on the Web, although participating in them isn't for everybody. It's sort of like the clinical trial of a medical treatment. The vendor thinks the new treatment is better or they wouldn't be testing it, but they might be wrong (or they wouldn't be testing it either, would they?) and sometimes are. If you like the thought of being a pioneer, of influencing new-product development like one of the families that allows the Nielsen company to record their TV-watching habits to compile ratings, then you'd probably like being a beta tester. On the other hand, if it made you feel like a guinea pig instead, you probably wouldn't. This means that the results of beta testing are always skewed toward early adopters and people who like technology. They tend to like powerful functionality more than the silent majority of users, and tend to care less about simplicity. It's hard for developers to learn what the silent majority thinks. Developers, therefore, need to shift the beta test results at least somewhat away from power and toward simplicity, as the U.S. census uses statistical methods to estimate the population that it can't actually reach.

In the preceding chapter, I discussed the Windows crash recorder, the piece of software that detects when a program crashes and sends the result to Microsoft for debugging. In that chapter, I spoke of the need to leave this crash recorder turned on. Think how much harder it would be to diagnose airplane accidents without crash recorders. They allow knowledge to come back from beyond the grave, too late to do any good for the people who produced it, but in time, hopefully, to save someone else. I hope you'll leave this turned on.

Speaking with my developer hat on, we know that it's much harder to put ourselves in our users' shoes than we initially thought. So *tell* us what's good and what's bad about our products.

3. RIDICULE

Never underestimate the power of ego, especially among computer geeks. Their image of themselves prizes intelligence over any other virtue. Looking stupid in front of their peers is their greatest fear, the nightmare that they'll work most diligently to avoid. That's why being included as a bad example in a book like this one, or being the subject of a "Hall of Shame" Web site like WebPagesThatSuck.com, has a large effect on a company. Managers and programmers get fired over this sort of thing.

The Internet makes it possible for individuals to make their voices heard much more widely than ever before. Almost every Web site that sells products allows users to write reviews of them, and I often consult these reviews when deciding which products to buy. For example, the reviews of one of my programming books on Amazon.com range from "superb and excellent introduction" to "I wanted to give it zero stars but Amazon wouldn't let me." There are a bunch of both types and not a whole lot in between, which gives potential buyers a good indication that it's a book you either love or hate. (Since you've made it almost to the end of this book, this bifurcation shouldn't surprise you much.) These reviews, right under a potential buyer's nose at the point of purchase, amplify the feelings of the previous users to a huge degree.

For example, I once bought my father an Internet stereo system for his birthday. It's a regular AM-FM-CD bookshelf stereo, except you can plug a broadband Internet connection into its back and use it to play music streams from the Internet (like RadioMargaritaville.com, Jimmy Buffett's online radio station). Unfortunately, it didn't work well and he wound up returning it.

The only positive outcome was that my mother allowed him to upgrade his Internet connection to broadband in order to run it, and then allowed him to keep it after he dumped the unit, and now enjoys the high connection speed at least as much as he does.

In the pre-Web days, that would have been the end of it: one annoyed customer, one returned item, but not much effect on anyone else. Today, though, he was angry enough to post a review on Amazon.com, which reads: "I was completely flummoxed by this complicated product with an absolutely impenetrable instruction manual. I have 3 college degrees, I consider myself computer literate, but this was beyond my imagination.... This product is made in China and I believe the instruction manual was written there also. Avoid this one like the Chinese plague." Another user wrote of the same product, "If you're a techno-geek, you love gadgets for their own sake, have plenty of cash to burn and plenty of hair left to pull out, go ahead and buy one of these just to say you did. Otherwise, wait until someone comes out with a better product that they are able to support." I'd say that the point has been made and Amazon will sell very few of these, wouldn't you? And in fact, the manufacturer has discontinued that product.

Ridicule, publicly, vendors that produce bad products. It gives you a wider reach and greater leverage. It feels really good, too. And while you're at it, don't forget to praise the good ones.

4. TRUST

You wouldn't spend $10 on a movie ticket without checking the reviews of that flick, so why would you do so for software, especially when you consider that you usually spend much more time with a program than with any movie, and that a bad movie can't steal your passwords and empty your bank account. You should make darn sure you investigate a potential program at least as diligently as you would a movie.

As different movie critics have different tastes, you quickly find which ones you agree with.[3] I've found that Walter Mossberg at the *Wall Street Journal* usually thinks along the same lines that I do (though somehow I doubt that's how he would phrase it). He values simplicity and ease of use as much as I do, as you can see in the opening line of his debut column many years ago: "Personal computers are just too hard to use, and it's not your fault." He has a taste for Macintoshes that I don't share. I also like Lee Gomes, who writes a different WSJ column, and David Pogue of the *New York Times* seems to have his head on straight. I also admire Jerry Pournelle, the science fiction writer and lead columnist at Byte.com, who may be too technical for readers of this book. He coined Pournelle's Law, which I've quoted many times and tried to follow in my own writing: "You can never have too many examples." There are many others, whom I'm sure you'll find once you start looking.

When you download and install software from the Web, you usually see a dialog box like the one in Figure 9–2, asking whether you trust the publisher and want to install the software. This is a useless and

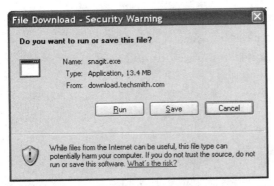

FIGURE 9-2 Useless, foolish, annoying waste of time that provides no safety whatsoever

---

3. The movie reviewer at the *Boston Globe* when I first moved to that town gave *Monty Python and the Holy Grail* only one star out of four. I quickly came to use his advice as a negative indicator—if he liked it, I wouldn't, and vice versa.

annoying waste of time that provides no safety whatsoever. If you know which vendor you want to trust, this mechanism ensures that it comes from them. But that's not the main question you ask when you surf the Internet. Instead, you usually wonder, "I never heard of this company until I Googled for [whatever]; now I'm reading their site and wouldn't mind trying their program, but I have no good way of determining whether to trust them." This box doesn't answer that question or even help in any meaningful way.

How can you possibly know enough to answer that question? You can't, you don't, and you never will. For programmers to depend on you to figure it out, or wash their hands of responsibility if you can't, are not acceptable responses in today's software environment. So how can you figure out who to trust online?

Mature industries have solved this problem by delegating the testing to a knowledgeable third party whom customers trust. For example, when you buy food labeled "organic," how do you know that it actually is? Unless you're an expert in food production and spend essentially all of your life examining food, you cannot reliably make such a determination yourself. Instead, you look for the certification seal from an agency you trust to have the specialized knowledge and perform the necessary inspections; for example, Oregon Tilth (www.tilth.org). Similar third-party certification programs exist for many qualities customers value but can't trust a manufacturer's claim for—wood from sustainably managed forests, fair trade coffee, food prepared according to a consumer's religious beliefs. The software industry needs to do something similar.

Software could be certified by either concentrated or distributed testing. The former would require a high-powered testing laboratory, conceptually similar to Underwriters Laboratories, which certifies electrical appliances in the United States. It would publish a code of best practices, such as using safe programming languages and requiring an acceptable privacy policy. It would then test applications for compliance with these standards and affix its digital seal to those that meet them. The lab would charge for this service, and the vendor would add the cost to the price of the application. Probably the mere fact of having to spend thousands on compliance testing would scare off most bad guys. Perhaps, to gain customer acceptance, the testing agency would offer some sort of insurance policy that would pay damages if the application turned out to be untrustworthy.

This concentrated model would leave smaller vendors out in the cold because they wouldn't be able to pay the fees. The alternative would be a distributed model, similar to the way that buyers rate sellers, and vice versa, on eBay. Customers who install an app could vote on whether it was trustworthy, and potential downloaders could examine the results of that vote when making their purchase decisions. It wouldn't help the very first users, and it wouldn't be infallible. But it would be pretty good, it would be easy to implement, and it would work for small vendors and even shareware. It'd be sort of like the Zagat restaurant review, which doesn't send its own critics to restaurants the way a newspaper does, but instead tallies the responses submitted by thousands of diners.

The system would have to be structured so that a bad guy couldn't rig it. Perhaps voting would be allowed only by numbered e-mail ballots sent to paid and registered customers. Maybe some public interest software foundation would run it, and maybe eBay or Amazon would donate the software as a sponsor opportunity. I propose the "Doesn't Suck Seal" for applications that pass. It'll feature a lollipop in a circle with a slash through it.

It's not enough to put these certifications on a Web site that users can look at, since no one ever does that. The final piece of this puzzle is to make the operating system pay attention to these third-party certifications, seamlessly downloading and installing applications that have them, and blocking those that don't. This has to be the job of the operating system manufacturers.

Until we have these testing programs in place, the best alternative is to find software reviewers that you *trust*, and follow their advice.

5. ORGANIZE

As anthropologist Margaret Mead (1901–1978) is credited with writing: "Never doubt that a small group of thoughtful, committed citizens can change the world; indeed, it's the only thing that ever has." The Internet has increased the power of individuals, yes. But far more than that, it helps individuals come together, coalescing into groups that can wield real power. That's a whole lot easier today now that everyone is online. For example, I doubt that alleged survivors of abuse by priests could have organized enough to force the Catholic Church into a settlement of their claims, in Boston and other cities, ten years ago, or even five.

Uniting into pressure groups and letting them fight it out in the marketplace is how modern society makes choices. Think about the American Civil Liberties Union or the National Rifle Association; Citizens for Responsible Growth and Citizens for Limited Taxation. These groups make a loud racket, file lawsuits, organize letter-writing campaigns and boycotts, lobby Congress, and sometimes even write legislation for overworked legislative staffers. Very few of them, however, deal with software, much less than you would expect given the ubiquity of software in our society. A number of groups deal with privacy rights, online and off, such as the Privacy Rights Clearinghouse (www.privacyrights.org) and Electronic Frontier Foundation (www.eff.org). But so far none of them has addressed the quality of software, at least not to my knowledge.

That needs to change, and you and I are going to make it happen. We need to use the power of today's Internet to make our voices heard about software quality. The more people that read a bad review, the harder the company who designed the product or Web site will work to avoid getting one. If I slam UPS.com, they think I'm a crackpot, too stupid to figure out their brilliant, intuitive user interface. But if we all slam them, maybe they'll get it through what passes for their brains that *they're* the ones who have it wrong, not us, and that they need to change. (So buy lots of copies of this book for your friends, OK?)

To achieve critical mass and leverage, I've formed Suckbusters, online at Suckbusters.com (see Figure 9–3). "Because Software Shouldn't Suck" is our motto. In a nod to the FBI's Ten Most Wanted list, I'm putting up the Ten Least Wanted pieces of sucky software. I need your help to do it. Send me the worst examples you can find, being as specific as possible. I'll try to keep it up-to-date. I'll put up links for sending e-mail to the manufacturers of such bad software. I'll also have a blog to discuss just why a particular piece of software sucks, and how it should work instead.

To paraphrase Arlo Guthrie in "Alice's Restaurant," if only I do it, people will think I'm crazy (but you knew that already). If three people do it, they'll think it's an organization. And if 50 people do it, they'll think it's a movement. And it will be. So come join me. And we'll make the software world into what it can be, should be, has to be.

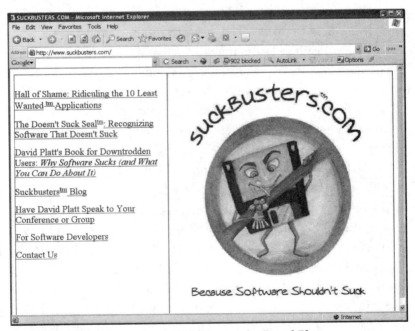

FIGURE 9-3 Suckbusters.com Web site, run by David Platt

You didn't know what improvements to ask for in your software, didn't even know that you *could* ask for improvements, and now you do. Five or six dozen feedbacks per day saying "Your language selection page is much harder than Google's, so fix it, and by the way, make this feedback form easier to get to" will get their attention. Taking your shipping business or coffee business or copying business to the companies that make their software and Web sites easy to use will hit the bad companies where it hurts. And posting bad designs on public halls of shame will rub the programmers' noses in their idoicy.

It's up to us, the customers, to make market demand work in software as it's worked in cars and banking and retailing. We can do it. Let's start. Now.

EPILOGUE

Thank you for reading this book. As software developers work for you, the customer, so I work for you, the reader. I know how busy you are, and I know how many other books call for your attention. I appreciate your sticking with mine. I hope you've found it worth your time. So thank you again. It would suck writing this book just for myself.

Watching my daughters grow up is bittersweet. I so dearly loved the one-year-old that ran on the beach in her peasant dress, and I won't ever see her again. The tags on their baby pajamas read, "If only they stayed small…" And yet, and yet, we all know better than to really wish for that.

The software industry is likewise growing up, and watching it is similarly bittersweet. Dang, did we have fun when all we had to worry about was rounding off the corners of the cards as they cascaded down at the end of a successful solitaire game. Now we have to shoulder the burdens of the world, as adults do. But as we do that, I hope we don't entirely lose that sense of playfulness as the industry matures, in the same way that I hope my daughters manage to keep some of it as they do.

As I have been blessed and honored to be present and to guide and to serve for their birth and childhood and, please God, their teen years and adulthood, so I have been blessed to be present at this moment in this industry. Not for its conception; that goes to giants like Alan Turing[1] and Jon von Neumann.[2] Nor for its child-hood; that goes to other giants like Admiral Hopper, whose first name so, so aptly was Grace.[3] But for its teen years, stormy as always, into maturity and adulthood. This belongs to me and my fellow geeks. To work and to guide and to serve.

And so, dear readers, until we meet again. Take care of your-selves. Take care of each other. And take it easy, but take it.

David S. Platt
Ipswich, Massachusetts
August 2006

---

1. Alan Mathison Turing (1912–1954) is credited with laying the mathematical foundations of computer science in his 1936 paper, "On Computable Numbers." He is best known to the general public for his contributions to the British efforts at cracking the German Enigma codes during World War II. He was convicted in 1952 of violating English laws against homosexual practices, causing him to lose his security clearance and be barred from his work. He committed suicide two years later by eating an apple coated with cyanide.

2. John Louis von Neumann (1903–1957) taught mathematics at the Institute for Advanced Study, where he was a colleague of Einstein and a professor of Turing. As part of the Manhattan Project during World War II, he developed important equations used for designing the Nagasaki bomb and most atomic weapons since then. To solve them in ever more complex weapon designs, he developed the basic architecture of the modern digital computer, still used in almost all computers built today. He seems to have predicted the modern geek mindset with his saying: "In mathematics you don't understand things. You just get used to them."

3. Grace Murray Hopper (1906–1992, a much better run than either Turing or von Neumann) earned a Ph.D. in mathematics from Yale in 1934. Her title is not a cour-tesy or nickname, as it is for some athletes. It is a rank (Rear Admiral of the Lower Half, if you want to get technical, pay grade O-7) which she earned on active duty in the United States Navy, beginning in 1943 and continuing on and off until her final retirement in 1986. She developed COBOL, the first modern programming lan-guage. Still in use today, primarily for business applications, it allows programmers to write programs using a syntax that resembles English. She is popularly credited with coining, in 1947, the term "debugging the computer" when she removed an electro-cuted moth (now on display in the Smithsonian Institute) from the Harvard Mark II Calculator (an early computer that used electromechanical relays). The U.S. Navy honored her in 1996 by naming an Arleigh Burke-class guided missile destroyer after her (USS Hopper, DDG-70).

ABOUT THE AUTHOR

 **David S. Platt** runs Rolling Thunder Computing (www.rollthunder.com), an education and consulting practice. He has more than twenty years of experience as a programmer, teaches software development at Harvard University Extension School and at companies all over the world, and is a popular speaker at conferences. He is the author of nine previous books—including *Introducing Microsoft .NET, Third Edition, The Microsoft Platform Ahead,* and *Understanding COM+* (all Microsoft Press)—as well as many journal articles and newsletters. In 2002, Microsoft designated him a Software Legend. Dave lives in Ipswich, Massachusetts.

HUMOROUS OUTRAGE

• • •

OUTRAGEOUS HUMOR

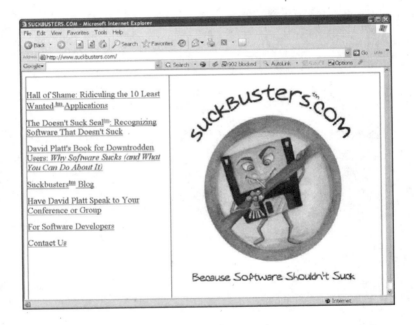

WWW.SUCKBUSTERS.COM